cators,
and everyone concern
row's world can learn exactly what one
of the nation's leading colleges is doing
and proposes to do to carry out its obligations.

A College Program in Action

A College Program in Action

A REVIEW OF WORKING PRINCIPLES
AT COLUMBIA COLLEGE

By the Committee on Plans

COLUMBIA UNIVERSITY PRESS
NEW YORK 1946

First printing May, 1946
Second printing June, 1946

Foreign agent: Oxford University Press, Geoffrey Cumberlege, Amen House, London, E.C. 4, England, and B.I. Building, Nicol Road, Bombay, India

Manufactured in the United States of America

Preface

As the title of this book implies, the following pages describe the actual functioning of a modern college long since dedicated to general education. This account is presented in the form of detailed self-criticism, the occasion for which was the common one of readjustment after wartime dislocation. Accordingly, here will be found discussed, in addition to curriculum, every sort of collegiate question from admissions policy to the degree with honors, and from faculty promotions to student extracurricular activities.

This inclusive report on a program and its application is addressed to two classes of readers—first, to our professional colleagues in other colleges and universities who face the same practical problems as ourselves, and who may find examples or suggestions, encouragement or solemn warning in seeing "how we do it." In particular, the outlines of our introductory required work in Contemporary Civilization, the Humanities, and the Sciences, printed very fully in Part Two, should serve a useful purpose. On these and other matters, the many inquiries received by the office of the Dean of Columbia College, both in my time and in that of my predecessor, H. E. Hawkes, show that a synoptic view of our offering and its administration supplies a continuing demand.

Secondly, this general review of our present performance is also addressed to the layman—the parent, prospective student, teacher in the schools, or general reader concerned with higher education. This book is, I may say, *confidently* addressed to him, though it was not specifically prepared for him. As a glance at page one will show, this text is simply a report made by a special committee to the Faculty of the College. It is reprinted here substantially as rendered, not groomed or trimmed for publication in any sense, except that after Faculty discussion of the proposals, alternative details of some were stricken out, and a few sentences alluding to familiar devices of instruction or administration were turned into sentences briefly explaining what these devices are.

My colleagues on the committee and I are convinced that the American public, which is taking such a lively interest in the question of higher education, and which has absorbed a good deal of literature from several qualified sources on that subject, is now ready to see for itself how one going concern carries out and keeps testing its own program for the education of college youth. The parent or student may at first experience some slight bewilderment at the number and kind of arrangements successively set forth; he may even be shocked to hear of defects freely acknowledged and seemingly baffling. But we believe that the reader who pushes on to the end will find the picture growing clearer and the role of the college more unmistakable. Indeed, we trust that he will gain and retain a fair notion of what a liberal arts college is like, and what it can do. This would seem to be, now and at any time, a desirable result, sparing those who want and those who give education from illusion and disillusion hereafter.

In presenting this report to the public, I feel it a pleasant duty to recall the fact that the Columbia College curriculum here anatomized is not the work solely of one mind, or one committee, or even one Faculty now in charge: it has been a collaborative enterprise which for a generation has drawn on the thought and energies of many men, some no longer in our midst. I have mentioned the late Dean H. E. Hawkes; let me add the names of F. J. E. Woodbridge, J. J. Coss, Rexford G. Tugwell, William E. Weld, and especially of John Erskine, whose inspired plan for reviving general education through the use of the great books has, since 1919, radiated from his seminar in Hamilton Hall to the four corners of the land.

Yet as each succeeding section of this report shows, we have no educational panacea to proffer, and we think we know that none exists. Our program is not perfect, even for our own designs; and we are quite sure that it cannot be adopted wholesale by other institutions. For one thing, we have learned that much depends on the efforts of a continually refreshed corps of devoted teachers. For another, we are conscious that real success comes from experience. This inevitably includes a shorter or longer span of trial and error, such as we have struggled through since the Faculty action of January 20, 1919, which resolved that "the requirement in Philosophy A and History A be replaced by a course in Contemporary Civilization."

Twenty-four years later, on the motion of Professor Horace Taylor, the Faculty voted in the midst of war that "the study of the liberal arts must not be permitted to languish during the existing national emergency . . . but must be pursued with great vigor and to as full an extent as the circumstances of war will permit." To the continuing body of that Faculty I tender my thanks for its contributions to this book, and even more for its faith in the liberal arts program which it is still building and perfecting on Morningside Heights.

HARRY JAMES CARMAN
Dean of Columbia College

Hamilton Hall,
April 15, 1946

Contents

THE PROGRAM

To the Faculty

Introduction

THE COMMITTEE ON COLLEGE PLANS reporting herewith was named in continuance of a committee appointed in July, 1943, by Acting Dean McKnight to consider a College policy for the years immediately following demobilization and the return of college students from war service. That initial committee believed that certain problems would require longer-range study than was called for in dealing with the postwar emergency and suggested the appointment of a new committee for the purpose. The new committee was identical with the one serving for the emergency. After it had begun its meetings, however, it lost to government service Chaplain Bayne and Professor Koopman, and subsequently added Professor Carman as Dean of Columbia College and also Professors Miner and Randall. There have been from the beginning to the present eleven members on the Committee, not more than nine sitting at any one time. The agenda has included probably every phase of curriculum and administration, and of faculty and undergraduate relationships.

Columbia College is far from standing alone in its concern for a program which shall be of the greatest possible service to the students of the future. The last three or four years have seen a general reappraisal of American college education, and widespread plans for reshaping curricula in response to needs revealed or created by our country's part in a world revolution. It is an exceptional college that has not undertaken a greater or smaller remolding of a hitherto acceptable program. War psychology has had much to do with what may at times seem like academic panic; that is certain. To a reasonable observer, however, it would seem that the disturbance and accelerated tempo of war years have simply brought closer to our consciousness the lag between the increasingly multiplex and complex intellectual movements of the recent past, and the natural and traditional conservatism of "higher" educational systems. Needless to say, this startled awareness of an accrued social debt to the community has been particularly concerned with the question of the relation of college education to the responsibilities of citizenship.

This report of the Committee on College Plans does not pretend to furnish an entire philosophy of higher education. It is first of all a study of the present state of health of Columbia College, with no dread of organic ills, hidden or public, but with concern that the educational regime accomplish all that it can possibly be made to accomplish. It is likewise a record. For the reestablishment of general education and the unifying of educational thought, which have gone forward so rapidly since the beginning of the Second World War, have been in progress within Columbia College experimentally for almost twenty-five years, and actively and affirmatively for more than a decade. We have a warrantable pride in the fact that the "new paths" that are opening before many of our best-known colleges are paths that we have first explored and then traveled with familiarity.

Beyond this examination of our present state, the report attempts to suggest means of bringing about greater coordination among policies and procedures for the realization of our declared principles. There is, for all these reasons, less discussion here of educational theories than of organization and practical means for the accomplishment of our purposes.

The work of your Committee has been in fact a fulfillment of views and policies already discussed at some length in the report of the Special Committee on Curriculum of 1935–36. The recommendations of the earlier committee affecting the plan of study in the upper college years, however, have not been put into complete practice or have been inadequately implemented, and (most important of all, perhaps) have never been brought within any framework of unified control. In some instances, therefore, what the present Committee has to recommend will recall similar proposals from the earlier committee. But we believe that the lapse of ten years or more has changed in some degree the complexion or the incidence of all these important problems.

The fundamental view of organization and policy submitted by the former Committee on Curriculum and accepted by the Faculty in 1936, was that a substantial part of the undergraduate work of the first two years should be devoted to orientation in the three studies which together describe the workings of the modern world: the humanities, the sciences, and the social sciences; and that the last two years should build upon this structure in a fashion flexible enough to recognize the matured capacities and interests of the particular student.

There is much room for debate whether the line of division between the first two and the last two years should be so sharp as to bring about two distinct types of study and academic life. Even though with us a "required course" does not imply standardized indoctrination, but only a common body of readings and topics for discussion, still there is no reason to doubt that a senior should be doing work of greater maturity, in type, range, and imaginative appeal. The present Committee is in accord with that view. It also supports the conclusion of the former committee that the pattern of general conformity in the work of the first two years should be replaced in the last two years by reasonably free election, and that this free choice should follow no uniform plan of synthesis, arbitrary unity, specialization, or other prescribed principle, but should be worked out in the best possible understanding of the particular student's needs and capacities.

It is of course clear that our objects with respect to the purpose and design of the first two years have now been realized through the courses in Contemporary Civilization, Humanities, and the Sciences. Your present Committee, while it suggests some minor changes in the first two of these courses, as well as in other matters of underclass instruction, feels that the plan of the freshman and sophomore work has plainly demonstrated its fitness for contemporary needs. It feels quite as strongly, however, that the important effort of the next few years must be the working out of plans for upperclass instruction.

So much for the setting in which your Committee has carried on its discussions. We have stressed these facts of background because our work has been essentially appraisal and clarification of what has been in process for almost the entire academic life of most of us. Our concrete proposals are therefore in the nature of corollaries to an already carefully studied, and in the main satisfactory, experience. Most of these proposals are implied in our more recent history; and there is little that will call for faculty action of a reconstructive sort.

On many questions your Committee has called upon special committees for study of the fields and interests involved. It has called also upon committees not appointed at the instance of the present Committee but already working upon related questions. The reports of these groups have served generally as the groundwork for your Committee's recommendations.

Admissions

ADMISSION STANDARDS and methods are of course basic in any attempt to measure the efficacy of our performance as a college. Yet for many years Columbia College has been satisfied to delegate almost all its responsibility for the policies and administration of this important service to a committee with only a secondary responsibility to the College itself—the University Committee on Admissions, consisting of the deans and directors of the various faculties. The day-to-day functions of that committee, moreover, are served wholly by appointive officers. For years the effective control of admissions into Columbia College has been exercised through these administrative officers, except when the Faculty has been called upon to deal with a question of policy originating in the Office of Admissions itself. Ordinarily, such proposed policies have received from the Faculty a somewhat perfunctory approval.

As a rule no member of the College teaching staff sees the applicant for admission, but only the enrolled student. Where analogy would suggest that the College have its own standing Committee on Admissions—as it has on Scholarships and on Instruction—the Faculty of the College is in practical effect without initiative and without an audible voice as to the first essential questions of student personnel: What kind of men do we want, and how can we pick them? Your Committee feels that this is a situation which should be remedied; and it can probably be remedied within the framework of the present statutes. There is ample precedent in the practice of other schools of the University for a committee on admissions representing the College Faculty.

The problems of admissions with which the Faculty of the College should be concerned are in the main those presented by a marginal group of applicants who fall within the category of "questionable risks"; for there is ordinarily small difficulty in recognizing a capable and desirable student, even if we assume that the admission of any and every student is in some degree a speculation.

But we must remember that a college of 1,800 men like ours, limited by space, staff, and laboratory facilities, cannot afford to pursue a policy of high speculation such as is possible to larger institutions accustomed to ridding themselves of academic failures on a heroic scale at the end of the first year. Moreover, our integrated program can be effective only if administered to men of a certain intellectual quality and moral fiber. The more we have abandoned instruction on the old magisterial lines, and the more we have encouraged self-direction in the use of mind and will power, the more we must seek out students who can feel at home in our classes and can profit from what we have to offer. Our small colloquiums and discussion groups must not be hampered in their operation by any large number of mere "spectators."

Your Committee therefore emphasizes the need of more searching procedures for dealing with marginal candidates or doubtful risks. It believes that the enlarged demand for college education within the next few years will offer an opportunity for the raising of entrance standards to a plane of unquestioned excellence. Yet it should not be assumed that the task of selection can be accomplished solely by examining the applicant's school record, or indeed by considering any one criterion of worth. The attempt to rely on a single decisive test of aptitude has, in the educational experimentation of the last two decades, invariably failed. In choosing our entrants, therefore, the Admissions Committee is bound to take into account—in addition to the formal records of study and deportment—character recommendations, evidence of interest in and familiarity with ideas, capacity for leadership, and signs of special talent. When it becomes necessary or desirable to choose between two or more candidates who have at least these basic qualifications, some of the determining considerations might be stated as follows:

1. Evidence of an established interest in science, literature, music, or art.

2. Evidence of having carried some worthwhile extracurricular activity through to some significant conclusion.

3. Evidence of having held responsible employment after school hours and during summers.

4. Ability to speak clearly and concisely and without affectation.

5. Manliness and directness of general manner.

6. Spontaneity and attractiveness of personality.

A policy of admissions is also bound to deal with the mooted question of geographical distribution, not indeed out of arbitrary feeling that the grass on the other side of the state line is greener, but out of a reasoned and widely shared conviction that college is an excellent place to bring together men from various sections of the country, no less than from foreign countries. It is a service, not only to those who come to us from distant parts, but also and especially to men of local origin, that this association of persons and points of view should take place. Both ideas imply the faith that mutual enlightenment and understanding are best achieved by living and learning together in the formative years of youth.

To give concrete embodiment to this belief, your Committee feels that experience over the past quarter century recommends a policy that should result in a student body composed approximately as follows: one third from Greater New York, one third from the metropolitan area within a 50-mile radius, and one third from remoter points, all these fractions to be slightly reduced to allow for students from foreign countries, who may be expected to seek admission after this war as they did before it.

It recommends also that a Standing Committee on Admissions for Columbia College be elected annually in a rotation similar to that of other standing committees, and that this Committee be called upon for personal service in the judgment and screening of applicants, particularly those on the fringe of eligibility.

The Committee also recommends that a written examination in English composition, given by Columbia College or by the College Entrance Examination Board or any other competent agency, be required of all candidates as indispensable contributory evidence of fitness for entrance.

Two questions of admissions policy affecting the relations of the high school and the college require notice. The first concerns a suggested means for relieving the heavy loading of required courses in our first two years, namely, giving widespread notice to prospective applicants that it is very desirable for them to secure high school credit in work anticipating some part of our first-year requirements. The obvious courses for the purpose are modern languages and advanced mathematics. Most high school courses of first-year college scope should have a negotiable value for incoming students, particularly for those whose programs are known from the outset to be crowded ones.

The second question is the outcome of much current discussion and some serious experimentation. It is whether we can, without injury to our standards and within the bounds set by the State Department of Education, admit students of promise who have completed three years, or possibly only two years, of normal high-school work. Such students would have a mixed status during their first year with us. That is, they would be taking some work on the high school level in University Extension to fulfill our requirements for admission, and they would also be taking some amount of work in the College itself. One university of standing has already adopted more radical concessions than those suggested here. There are of course arguments of weight both for and against the suggestion, but it is an expedient already in fairly reputable practice. We should watch the results of such attempts and be ready to give fair consideration to their applicability here.

Over-All Organization

COLUMBIA COLLEGE has given great attention over the last twenty-five years to its expanding plans for fundamental instruction, during the lower two years, in Contemporary Civilization, the Humanities, and the Sciences. Moreover, by requiring sixty "maturity credits" for the degree, the college has sought to prevent a student's graduating (as Dean Hawkes used to put it) "after four years of freshman work." Your Committee believes, however, that it is not enough to prevent a student from using most of his mental energy in the avoidance of difficult courses. There still remains the necessity of getting him to recognize the value of a consistent mental discipline, a discipline consistent in one of a number of possible ways.

With this problem in mind, the previously mentioned Committee of 1936 proposed a fairly clear line of cleavage between the first two undergraduate years and the last two. Doubtless that proposal received more stress than it deserved. Our first two years, it is true, are taken up with the requirements of the introductory courses, a foreign language,

English, and physical education, and there is a visible difference between these lower years and the almost completely free election in the junior and senior years. The pressure of required courses upon underclassmen will be still more marked if the Faculty adopts the recommendations of the present Committee for a tightened requirement in Humanities B, more directly profitable language instruction, and a broader and more consistent attention to reading and the use of the spoken and the written word, no longer to be regarded as an isolated performance for "English class." These changes would limit freedom of election in the first two years somewhat more than at present. The encroachment, however, does not seem a serious one—of which more in its proper place.

Within the discussions of your Committee it has been remarked that a good student throughout the first two years not infrequently slumps in his junior year, less, perhaps, because of jaded intellectual appetite than because of an excess of mental energy that might be put to work in courses with an activity and spread which would appeal to his maturer needs. A course built upon an introduction to economics or chemistry may nevertheless not be a distinctively upperclass course. Course C, which follows Course B, which in turn follows Course A, may be simply more of the same thing. The assignment of maturity credits to certain continuation courses has sometimes failed to meet the actual situation adequately. We need a redefinition of what it is we expect from juniors and seniors. We assume that upperclass courses should increase in importance and difficulty, but not merely by our stressing their importance and making them difficult. They should appeal to a developed imagination, encourage independent effort, and develop articulateness, not merely deepen the channels of accustomed labor. It has been mentioned within the Committee that the science sequences, the English three-year sequence, the Colloquium on Important Books,* and the senior seminars seem to have realized most of these aims, but the Committee believes that we still offer upperclass courses in which results are measured too much by a student's absorptive capacity and not enough by his enlightenment.

To sum up, in our system the work of the first two years is a standard discipline for all students; the work of the second two years should be based by careful design upon the work of the first years. Schemes of convenient but random elections are out of place in an institution which has put as much serious effort into foundation work as we have. For the question follows: Foundation for what?

The former Committee on Curriculum answered this question by proposing three acceptable types of upperclass work: (1) general, but not random, study for a student who wants to expand his knowledge within a wide circle of genuine interests; (2) work that is largely within a field of related interests but is not "professionally" directed; and (3) specialization of any degree of concentration that the student's mind can properly command. It would be idle to regard any of these plans of study as better or worse than any other, except in respect to a particular student's aims and capacities. But it is essential that a student's aims and capacities should be brought into relation with what he

---

* For a description, see below, pp. 164–171.

wants to undertake. That calls for an advisory system which, while avoiding both coddling and compulsion, will offer the proper kind of aid to a young man standing at this critical point of choice.

Obviously, then, there should be a "screening" of all our students at the end of their second year. Such a screening should utilize the academic record, definite judgments of promise from instructors or departments, personal estimates from instructors, the student's own appraisal of his work and needs, and any other available sources of knowledge and opinion. And the results of such a screening should reach the instructors and the departments interested in the student's future. The screening would also furnish an opportunity for final decisions upon students whose grip upon the railing of intellectual life seemed weak. There are probably men, not necessarily men who have had frequent summonses to the Dean's office, for whom two years of college have been salutary but not greatly rewarding, and for whom two more years could do little more than prolong mediocre performance. In such cases our responsibility is to preserve by the screening process the quality and effectiveness in the work of the upper college.

The advisory system to be introduced for the upper classes should serve somewhat different ends from those achieved by our present advisers, the Assistants to the Dean. We do not suggest that the present advisory system be replaced; in fact we feel that the adviser appointed for each student in his freshman and sophomore years should continue in this relation during the junior and senior years; for it would be wasteful to break so serviceable a contact. The advisory system for the upper classes, however, should have regard to the particular usefulness that a department or a field of study may have for a particular student. And while the appointment of upperclass advisers for this purpose would be by departments (or in some cases by divisions) of the College, there should be some permanent relation established among the advisers appointed for this purpose, and some definition of collective policies and procedures. Probably the practice of the committee now in charge of our Colloquium on Important Books would offer many useful leads for the organization of these responsibilities. Your Committee believes that the upperclass advisory group could, once appointed, find its own way through these problems, which are stated here only in general form. The need of a wider and better integrated advisory program for the upper classes appears indispensable for any scheme of serious and mature work in the later years.

As for the upperclass courses themselves, we believe that no single type of course or method of instruction has any preeminent claim to be the best or the most mature. The former Committee on Curriculum recommended an increase in the number of seminars and colloquiums, but there is evidently room for lecture courses, readings courses* with reduced hours of actual classroom or conference work, and, naturally, graduate courses for students clearly prepared to profit by them. During the last few years all these types of courses have entered increasingly into upperclass work, but we have probably not yet reached the rational limit of elasticity in the number and variety in this part of our offer-

* For descriptions, see below, pp. 161 ff.

ing, especially in interdepartmental offerings. Initiative in this matter must obviously come from the separate departments, some of which have already set a very liberal example.

The tendency in this type of reorganization of upperclass college work is mainly toward smaller groups under instruction; toward the staffing of courses of limited size by two or more cooperating instructors, chosen occasionally from more than a single department; and toward more exacting tutorial and advisory responsibilities The net effect of these changes is a redistribution of the time and effort put into instruction, at a relatively higher cost. But this expense must be met if Columbia College is to fulfill its opportunity, particularly as one of the colleges within the intellectual shelter of a great university.

Your Committee is not unanimous as to the desirability of comprehensive or divisional examinations at the end of the senior year, particularly for those students who elect to work within some field of specialization. A *majority,* however, favors such examinations, whether divisional or departmental, because of their usefulness in tying together the related subjects taken up in four years of study, and in dissipating the darkness of the compartmented mind. The minority has taken the position that a final examination might fail to accomplish what four years of instruction had failed to accomplish, and that the real remedy for a possible lack of integration should be found in better-planned instruction. There are at any rate two questions to be honestly faced before deciding affirmatively on this proposal: Does the staff want to undertake the heavy burden of preparing and reading such examinations? And is it willing to "break" a candidate for a degree if he fails to show capacity for comprehensive thinking at the end of his four years with us?

The question of the meaning of a degree with honors is obviously attached to many of the matters that we have considered in connection with the upper College, but we have preferred to deal with it as a separate item in another place. (See p. 54.)

Consideration was also given to a senior course in "synthesis," as a requirement having retrospective and summary purposes. The upshot of rather lengthy discussion was that if our whole plan of instruction does not offer a synthesis, then we have failed in our central purpose. Moreover, such a course (still considering it as a requirement) would be possible and profitable only under a more or less authoritarian academic code; but where the spirit of instruction is grounded rather in pragmatic liberality, it would not seem to be an essential part of a well-ordered scheme of instruction. It might be useful as an elective, given, presumably, by the Department of Philosophy. The position of your Committee, however, is here the same as with respect to required comprehensive examinations in the senior year—that large-scale syntheses, reviews, and résumés of any sort may have a highly valuable place in the purposes of a department or division, which might adopt any design of this sort it thought proper; but there is probably too much variety of matter and method within our whole field of instruction to make it wise for us to standardize our upper-college procedures explicitly and compulsively.

The Liberal Arts Program

IT IS no lip service to tradition to declare once more that the liberal arts program should be the heart of our interests and aims as a college. In the meaning of liberal arts we include all studies that contribute to the art of living, as distinct from the channeled preparation for making a living. What we gladly concede to the necessities of "preprofessional" education leaves us still convinced that the student for whom we can do most and who can do most for us is the four-year liberal arts student. This conviction is supported in the admissions practices of our very best professional schools, which have gone more and more definitely on record as preferring a candidate with a well-rounded four years of college work to the candidate who has worked more assiduously upon useful but narrow preparation for his profession. Our own students who are going into medicine and law become in increasing numbers candidates for a "straight" A.B.

Yet we still devote time and energy to our preprofessional programs and to one- or two-year preparatory programs for men going into Architecture, Engineering, and the School of Business. To the extent that the distinctive Columbia College plan of the first two years contributes to the awakening and enlightenment of these students' minds, the effort is obviously well spent. It often happens that starting with a determination to "work off" academic requirements in the most perfunctory manner, so as to reach his vocational work with the least delay, a student in our Humanities or Contemporary Civilization course learns there a different attitude towards life and towards his own mind. Financial conditions permitting, he changes his plans to include an additional year or two of liberal arts, and sometimes he shifts his professional interest altogether. The value of our basic requirement for all underclassmen is here apparent: the man who shifts in mid-career is not penalized or forced to make a fresh beginning.

Professional Options

OUR professional options—three years of college work leading to the A.B. degree at the end of the first additional year in professional school—should be a healthful union of serious general education with later specialization opening into a professional field. We know from experience that the pattern of our first two years of work can be adapted to these special needs—as well as to the needs of specializing students, such as science majors, who are not going forward to strictly professional degrees. There is no specialized sequence of studies in our offering to which the program of the first two years cannot be accommodated. What concessions have to be made in mere scheduling can be made without regret, for the seriousness and generally good tone of preprofessional students and specializing students working for the degree make them on the whole desirable undergraduates.

Combined Programs

A "COMBINED PROGRAM" is within our own definition and practice an arrangement of courses planned to give, generally within two years, the minimum essentials for admission to a school of the University which is not on the graduate footing. The problems connected with these courses, and with the students who take them, are quite distinct from those presented by the preprofessional courses. The students in the combined courses constitute the group for whom the greater part of the compromises with the customary program of requirements must be made.

The Committee's views respecting these combinations of courses can be put simply and briefly. We think that such courses interfere with most of the educational objects we respect, and we hope that the schools which they serve will in not too distant a time come to share our belief that a homeopathic college preparation is not a good one for any vocation that claims professional standing and exerts great influence in the modern world. The liaison between the College and these schools has too often resembled what the nurseryman calls an "unsympathetic graft," and we therefore see only two ways in which this undesirable condition may be altered. The first is a change in the psychology of this intramural relationship, which in the long run would mean the establishment of the quasi-professional schools of the University as actual graduate and professional schools; the second is the transfer of service courses to a division of the University that will give value received to a student who desires "points," but who cannot, or does not wish to, submit himself to the risks of broader cultivation.

The Introductory Courses

THE introduction of orientation courses in Columbia College, with the establishment in 1919 of the course in Contemporary Civilization, was the beginning of a quiet and gradual revolution in undergraduate instruction throughout the United States. Although a number of colleges are still weighing the idea of requiring introductory courses so planned as to acquaint the student with the framework of Western culture, yet the dissemination of the idea has been very wide; and its use as a basic formula by many of our most important colleges and universities in the present reexamination of curricula is evidence of the depth to which it has influenced higher education in this country.

Experience has shown that full and free cooperation among departments is necessary to make this aim a practicable one. Our introductory course in the sciences, established in 1934, attempted the task in its most difficult aspect, and has undergone revisions the most recent of which is described on a later page. In 1937 the course in Humanities—an offshoot of Professor Erskine's Honors Readings in Great Books—rounded out the now familiar introduction to world literature by providing in the second year an introduction to the special idioms of music and the fine arts. Together, the three two-year sequences in science, the social sciences, and the humanities have brought us, we believe, to the point at which the younger student is offered a comprehensive view of what goes to the making of an intelligent citizen of the world. The salutary influence of these courses upon the mental consciousness and capacities of our students has been accepted by all but an almost negligible minority of the students themselves; and the merging of previously divided interests in the departments of instruction, as well as the broadening effect of this merging upon the instructors who have conducted the courses, are probably results of no less importance to the well-being of college education.

If the introduction to science, which has hitherto been an alternative to departmental courses in the first two years, is to be required of all undergraduates, the three introductory courses will take up 44 points of the 124 now required for graduation—about 35 percent of the student's whole obligation to the College, and well over half of the freshman and sophomore programs. Some departments still feel that so great a claim may obstruct a student's well-considered educational plans and defer the building up of sequences of study in certain branches of undergraduate specialization. But in actual administration, adjustment or postponement of a part of the orientation work has eliminated serious difficulties of this kind, and there is no reason to believe that the future will present more serious problems than the past.

The test of experience in teaching these orientation courses in Columbia College strengthens our belief that they are not the place for the display of personality in the form of lectures to student audiences large enough to fill a theatre. For many years we have given in Columbia College no required courses of the pontifical type, in part because the students know the defects of the type, but principally because the man-to-man effectiveness of a proved instructor, young or old, with a small group—usually twenty or twenty-five—has had much to do with active undergraduate interest in the introductory work, and with the easy and steady improvement of the courses themselves.

THE INTRODUCTION TO CONTEMPORARY CIVILIZATION

This course, as has been noted, is the highly respected grandparent of all the "orientation" courses. It was organized in 1919 to explain issues growing out of the recent war, through the pooling of the interests and claims of the departments of history, economics, government, and philosophy. Since that time it has changed in scope and form, but not in aim. It began as a five-hour-a-week course, given throughout the freshman year, and it now requires four hours weekly in the freshman year and three in the sophomore.

Twenty-five years of examination and reexamination of the results in "C.C." have brought the course to a high degree of standardization, without prejudice, we believe, to the initiative of individual instructors. Its program is so perfectly familiar to both undergraduates and the great number of our graduates that it seems unnecessary here to discuss the course further. Other readers will find a fairly detailed description of its contents and methods on pp. 95–103 of this book.

THE INTRODUCTION TO THE HUMANITIES

The Humanities course has united the interest of all the departments concerned with literature (in the most extensive sense), music, and the fine arts. At various times it has employed instructors in philosophy, history, English, music, the fine arts, Greek and Latin, French, German, Italian, and religion. When the course was brought into the curriculum in 1937, only the first year (readings in literature, philosophy and history from Homer to Goethe) was a fixed requirement. The second year (a term each of music and fine arts) could be replaced by approved courses in literature, philosophy, or other related subjects. Throughout the history of the course this privilege of fairly free substitution has been gradually reduced, though even now only a minority of our sophomores take the second-year course in music and fine arts, Humanities B.

Experience in the giving of both Humanities A and Humanities B, however, has convinced the staffs of both courses that their subject matter should reach all our students without exception. The reasons which at first deterred the Departments of Music and of Fine Arts from urging this step were, first, that they would for some time confront difficulties in staffing, and, second, that they were not convinced that prepossessions and "blind spots" would not present insuperable difficulties in the path of student achievement. Both of these doubts have by now been put to rest. The departments and the Faculty are ready to go forward and test their belief that the methods of staffing and instruction for Humanities B can now be easily brought into line with the rest of our introductory program. The revised outlines of this course (pp. 110 ff.) carry clear a presumption of the experiment succeeding.

It should be noted in passing that an important stimulus

to the spirit underlying the instruction in the Humanities, as in Contemporary Civilization, is the weekly luncheon, not only of the staff but of the numerous friends of the course. These luncheons are on occasion "business luncheons," but for the greater part they are simply natural and friendly exchanges in a group of highly diverse men with interest in a common object. Men from many departments and others from the administrative staff have sat with the group, neither to learn nor to instruct, but to talk and laugh.

The suggestions coming from a student group which has considered some of the questions here discussed included a proposal to extend Humanities A into a third term, covering the nineteenth and twentieth centuries. The merit of the proposal, apart from its practicality, probably calls for no argument. But the criticism implied was fairly faced from the very beginning of the discussion of a required course in the Humanities; and the question was settled by recognizing that the readings for Humanities A should be books of established eminence. There is for us no question as to the place in the history of European culture of Sophocles, of Dante, or of Voltaire. We have not yet a similar perspective for Carlyle or Nietzsche or Freud.

In the second place, tradition has an importance for the humanist which is not so evident for the psychologist, the economist, or the scientist. Homer is still a great writer, though his society has been dead for centuries; but a student of government today takes Aristotle's *Politics* as a philosophic appraisal of human relations, not as a guide to modern politics. The astronomer, meanwhile, can feel little more than antiquarian interest in the Ptolemaic view of the heavens. In other words, in the humanities the living record goes back to the very beginning. In the social sciences and in the pure sciences the central concern is the present state of society, social and intellectual. The stopping point for Humanities A was accordingly taken to be the period, about 1800, after which the application of literary canons becomes more uncertain and the flux of ideologies more confused. Mindful also of the fact that the pressure of time obliges a cut somewhere, the organizers of the course thought it best to cut transversely at the year roughly indicated. But the demand for a sequel to embrace the works of the century and a half since 1800 is well defined and fully justified, and it has been met by the offering of an appropriate elective, beginning in 1946–1947.

THE INTRODUCTION TO THE SCIENCES

Into this plan of orientation courses it has been found very difficult to introduce a course in general science conceived in the same over-all fashion as the courses in Contemporary Civilization and the Humanities. It would seem that if the departments of history, philosophy, and economics could, in the interest of intellectual coordination, surrender or modify their claims on student time, then the science departments should face no serious difficulties in organizing a similarly unified course in general science. But the proposal, frequently brought before the Faculty, has met opposition—for the greater part from the science departments themselves. What has underlain that opposition, if we interpret it correctly, is not the wish to preserve "vested interests," but a set of general convictions that embrace these particular points: (1) that a course of even as much as 16 term hours out of 124 required for graduation must fail to touch more than the surfaces of subjects such as chemistry, physics, and biology, (2) that the approaches and techniques of the separate sciences can scarcely be fused into a single point of view and a single method, (3) that the problem of staffing such a course would be all but insuperable, because the degree of specialization necessary to make an instructor an accomplished teacher of physics or chemistry would almost *ipso facto* prevent his being an equally competent instructor in biology and geology, (4) that the road to a teaching career in the scientific fields, particularly in a large university, is high serviceableness in a single domain of study, or at most in a domain which focuses the relations of two cognate sciences. Few young instructors, therefore, would care to scatter their energies in instruction that would not be highly regarded by the department to which they owed their primary responsibility. (5) Particularly for students in the sciences such a general course could have no effective articulation with "serious" courses in the particular sciences, and what a student specializing in the sciences might gain in perspective would be offset by his having no adequate foundation for continued work in any given science.

Two successive efforts have been made at Columbia in the last three decades to breach this impasse: the late Professor Barry's elective lecture course in the History of Science (to be staffed and offered anew beginning in 1946–1947); and the collaborative two-year course established in 1934. This also was an alternative to the choice of specific courses in particular sciences which could fulfill the science requirement, and it has never been taken by anything like a majority of the students facing that requirement. The course, however, has been in the large view successful, even though its unity and the comprehensiveness of its purpose have been perhaps obscured in some degree by the fact that it is still in large measure a departmentalized course, an instructor in physics teaching physics, and an instructor in geology, geology.

Your Committee, therefore, has from the beginning of its meetings looked upon an integrated and thoroughly collaborative required introductory course in the sciences as an extremely important desideratum. Every effort, we felt, should be made to find a design conformable to our general plan of instruction and also acceptable to self-respecting teachers of the sciences. Very special care was taken that in the selection of the subcommittee for this purpose not only every department concerned should be represented, but every facet of opinion as to the policies involved.

The subcommittee has considered all the current objections to such a course from teachers of science, and it has proposed a plan that the majority of its members believe to be educationally profitable and practicable. The majority of the subcommittee has brought in a report in favor of a course planned not merely as an introduction to the several sciences, but as a serious and exacting discipline in the logic and the methods of the scientific worker.

At an earlier stage in the discussion of this subcommittee it was proposed that an orientation course in science should be required of all students except those who planned from the first to specialize in either technology or theoretical science. Further consideration, however, approved the course as a requirement for all students, on the ground, in the first place, that the absence from the course of the best qualified and most interested students would prove a deterrent to the energy and interest of the others, and more importantly still, that the very students who specialized in science would otherwise lose an over-all view of the relations of their subject to the entire field of scientific and philosophic inquiry.

To the practical objection that sixteen hours taken from the first two years of study for students in the sciences would interfere with the sequence of specific courses (such as mathematics and physics, for students in chemistry) which establish the foundation for concentrated work in science in the last two years, the subcommittee answers that, in the first place, these sequences can be taken in the first two years simultaneously with the orientation course, if freshman and sophomore courses are rebalanced for the purpose, and that, in the second place, if an orientation course in science is adopted, the science departments should adapt their entire programs of undergraduate work to the introductory course as the foundation for their later instruction.

So much serious effort has gone into this inquiry, and so many practical questions have been faced, that your Committee on Plans regards the current proposals as an excellent opportunity to apply the test of practice by the prompt setting up of the general course proposed. A project involving so many problems of selection and balance must entail compromises. No one can be wholly satisfied with all that is either included or omitted. But your Committee is confident that the plan now laid before the Faculty has mapped out the field of introductory teaching in the sciences to the greatest possible advantage, and has reconciled some of the main differences of perspective and judgment which have seemed in the past to stand as unsurmountable obstacles. Divergences of opinion which may remain can doubtless be compromised in the same spirit when the detailed syllabus comes to be worked out. A brief account of the original course and a statement of the principles proposed for the new will be found on pp. 116–138 of this book.

Other Required Courses

THE FOREIGN LANGUAGES

Possibly nothing has prejudiced the approach to and the spirit of the undergraduate's study of foreign languages more than the idea current in recent years that the principal, if not the only important, use of language study is as a "tool" to serve general education. So far as that view has been reflected in our own institution, it can be regarded as little less than disastrous. It may even be seriously doubted whether so limited a role for language can achieve its own limited object, stressing as it does, and must, mere "reading knowledge" of the most superficial and imprecise sort. For any worth-while result in the study of a foreign language, certainly the language must be regarded as a source of knowledge and pleasure; and the elements of study must include ability to distinguish sounds and to reproduce meanings in the foreign tongue.*

The measure of achievement in a foreign language has been for many years, in our practice, a proficiency test. Clearly this should be a more valid proof of competence than any number of courses "taken." Yet the results have not been satisfactory, very likely because this test is a test only for the eye; not for the tongue and the ear. It has also been criticized by members of the modern language departments as directed too much to vocabulary and not sufficiently to construction and to the literary sense. Many members of these departments have steadily refused to admit the efficacy of these tests even for their declared objective—establishing the minimum "useful" proficiency in the language.

The recent war has given us a convincing and large-scale demonstration that highly intensive language study may yield extraordinary returns in relation to the period spent upon it. This is not quite the educational revelation that many have taken it to be; for similar plans have in the past met with consistent success in private language schools. And in judging the well-publicized efficiency of the language instruction set up by the United States Army and Navy, certain conditions must be taken into account that it might be difficult to parallel, or approximate, in even the best colleges. The Army instruction was organized exclusively for the one purpose—rapid mastery of a single lan-

---

* One member of the Committee dissents from this entire view of the proper aim of foreign language study.

guage, with the essential aspects of the culture it represents. All collateral work was closely related to language instruction; oral use of the language was insisted upon from the earliest moment in all of the student's daily concerns; and the time spent in this language instruction was generally greater than the total course requirements in the average college. Moreover, the students in these schools were selected for proved aptitude in language study; they were volunteers with a strong interest in the program; and they worked under a spiritual as well as a rational stimulus far more intense than the diversified mental activities of the normal student in college.

Yet the record of success remains, and has lent encouragement to the view that similar methods in undergraduate instruction would produce comparable successes. Many colleges, no doubt, will borrow from this type of organization and these techniques in the overhauling of their own language instruction. Some in fact have already announced their intention of doing so, and plan to devote a substantial part of the first-year schedule to the intensive process.

A committee from the Departments of German and French has reported a plan for an intensive elementary language course (for description, see p. 143) which is to be made available to students in Columbia College. The program calls for ten hours a week of classroom work, with six points of academic credit each term. Though the course is recommended, and with the best of justification, for freshmen, it would raise the program of any regular student to at least 21 points in his first term, a load that the deans and the advisers regard as quite impossible for most freshmen.

For a student having to build up a progression of special courses as a foundation for upperclass specialization (for example, the science student) it would be completely out of the question. It would be practicable, however, for some sophomores, and entirely practicable—if we modified our maturity credit requirement—for juniors and seniors wishing to master a second language.

It has been suggested that our concern over heavy freshman programs is paternalistic, and that the average freshman or sophomore in the College possesses a capacity for effective work substantially in excess of what we encourage. If that is so, a 21-point program including a 6-point intensive language course might be risked, experimentally, with students who come to us with excellent high school records. But this possibility affects the whole question of scheduling for the lower classes, and may be discussed in relation to any combination of subjects, not only in relation to the intensive language course.

As the situation stands, a 6-point language course would be available only to the freshman who by an achievement test had cleared his schedule of one of the required introductory courses. Such cases are so rare that they are almost negligible. No doubt, then, the student who undertakes elementary language study in his freshman year will have to be content with a less accelerated course carried through two years. What may be learned from the organization and methods of the army language schools should, of course, be turned to profit in our less intensive courses. The Committee feels that this problem, and the related one of providing students with parallel opportunities for the study of French or German or Spanish, should be entrusted as a special duty to the language departments. In view of these changed conditions, the departments concerned should reappraise their offerings, their staffs, and their methods, so as to insure a more comprehensive command of foreign languages than we have achieved in the past.

One other possibility remains for the use of an intensive language course. At the moment the College staff feels that continuous year-round sessions are a delusion and a danger. Yet when we have once forgotten the strain set up by the needs of the war period, we may feel free to consider our long summer vacation as a reservoir of special opportunities for the students who would value them. If we again offer ten- or twelve-week summer courses, perhaps one of the most clearly profitable would be a college course devoted exclusively to the study of a single language, given preferably out of the city and with recreational opportunities at hand. Student opinion has been canvassed on this project, and the response has been not merely favorable but animated.

ENGLISH COMPOSITION

With the cooperation of the Department of English your Committee has studied the problems of the student in the use of the written and the spoken word, and the measures, both traditional and potential, for dealing with them. The findings of the Committee on this question involve a complete restatement of principles and the proposal of a plan which may seem in some respects radical, but which is in fact as old as the university system itself.

Historically, the writing of the vernacular (or, in earlier years, of Latin, the scholarly vernacular) was an explicit, pervasive, and undisputed part of the scholar's general training. It was a specific subject of study under the name of rhetoric, but it was the container and the medium of all intercourse in all subject matters, and its discipline was inseparable from any and every field of instruction. In that sense, as a measure of the aptitude and responsiveness of the student in every field of effort, it was everybody's concern. And that concern was exercised, as it is today in the English and French universities, by teachers in history, in philosophy, or in mathematics, who refused to accept ill-considered and slovenly writing from students who should be capable of better.

About the middle of the nineteenth century, in the American universities particularly, "rhetoric" came to be regarded as a separate subject of instruction, and its accepted aim came to be, not the training of the mind for the general purposes of communication and discussion, but the development of a special proficiency, rightly or wrongly identified with "literature." There is probably little reason to doubt that the refinements of writing received better attention under that plan; it is much more questionable whether they affected more than a small minority of the students exposed to them. But it is quite certain that the final effect of the plan was to delegate the sole responsibility for writing as a general discipline to a department—usually a department of "English" or of "composition"—which could not exert its influence effectually beyond the doors of its own classrooms.

Any delegation of a responsibility must assume the reasonableness of the commitment and the capacity of the agent to perform the undertaking. But the commitment in this case was never reasonable if it implied that writing was anything less than a serious discipline reaching into the remotest recesses of academic effort. And the agent was never competent for the purpose if the aims of instruction were to lose their relation to the requirements of a general discipline. Almost inevitably the system deteriorated. Having delegated the responsibility, college teachers came to feel that they had no share in it, and brought neither authority nor interest to bear upon the student's performance as it affected them. In effect, the average professor said, "These students are in your hands now. You make them write. I am concerned with facts, with categories, processes, methods; expression doesn't concern me. If the student knows the facts, the form is external and unimportant."

Quite as inevitably the student has taken his cue from the attitude of his instructors. As a rule he regards English as an isolated study with its own objectives, which for some mysterious reason he is required to take in his freshman year. When he is through with it, he is through. His formal debt to a department has been paid. He is held to no further obligation; so he recognizes none. His performance may reach depths of obscurity and carelessness, but he will never be called to account for it; so why should he worry?

In the United States at this time the problem is much more serious than it could be under any circumstances in a European country with a relatively homogeneous culture, no great diversity of language backgrounds, a sense of the integrity and dignity of the spoken tongue, and an efficient lower-school instruction in writing conveyed by teachers with a powerful pride in all of these conditioning facts. The American secondary-school system is built upon no such proved foundation for language instruction and practice. And our colleges, therefore, have had passed on to them the deficiencies of both a diversified culture and an imperfect school system.

What is essential, then, in the very approach to this question is a restatement of the balance of relationships and responsibilities between the English Department and the other departments in the College. We must use powerful and insistent moral pressure to break down the feeling among students that composition is only a subject, and that it has no important connection with any other subject. We must overcome the unwillingness of many departments to regard the qualities of their students' writing as significant determinants of standing in their courses, and the prevalent tendency to pass on to the English Department the blame for not "making them write." In the British universities every paper written is judged not merely for "content," but for ineptitudes of expression and defects in organization. For the connection of clarity of expression with clarity of thought is a matter of central importance. What is clearly thought out can generally be expressed; if expression fails, then facing the problems of coherent speech is for the student one of the first means of clarifying thought. Conversely, there is no better "matter" for training in composition than that which is provided daily in the discipline of most courses. But writing does not take care of itself, no matter how fruitful for the purpose the content of even the best of courses. The writing must be viewed as writing, and must be subjected constantly to interested criticism.

We recognize, however, that the long divorcement of instruction in composition from general instruction has produced in both instructors and students, attitudes and habitudes that are not going to be broken down quickly either by sound educational precept or by forms and regulations meant to broaden our collective responsibility. What is immediately possible in extending that sense of responsibility can be discovered only by enlisting, as a first step, the cooperation of the instructors most concerned with the necessities of articulate communication in the freshman year, namely, those who teach the courses in Humanities A and Contemporary Civilization A. We wish those instructors to recognize the urgency of the problem and the propriety of our demanding their interest in it. We propose that the responsiveness of the student be judged in these courses by a steady requirement of written work, to be criticized both as to command of the material of the course and as writing. If it is argued that the effects of such a proposal will be to dilute the subject matter of the course, we suggest that the ultimate subject matter of every course is the brain of the man who takes it. More frequent writing should clarify the results of instruction and bring subject matter more definitely within the range of usable experience.

We recommend also that our administrative policy be used to give force to the requirement of careful and presentable writing by embodying it in the standards of every course given in the College, even to the extent of making it, in critical cases, the determinant of passing or failing.

The Committee proposes a one-year course of instruction in composition during the first year, meeting two hours a week, but counting as one point of credit each term (the equivalent in hours and credit of the present requirement in English C). This course should comprise remedial instruction in mechanics; discussion of organization, phrasing, words, and their uses, (relying in part for practice in these regards upon the actual written work of the courses in Contemporary Civilization and Humanities); and independent work in composition, a substantial part of it impromptu. It must be understood that if we continue to admit students untrained or undisciplined in writing, the Department will be obliged to continue segregating these students in order to deal with their problems on a lower level of instruction, as at present, without credit. But exemption from the required course must also be given to students whose capacities warrant it, on the assumption that with proper attention to written work in the cooperating courses they will have ample opportunity to practice writing. The detail of these proposals will be found below, on pp. 146–154.

PHYSICAL EDUCATION AND HYGIENE

Though we occasionally hear an admission from a student that health and physical tone have their importance in enabling him to carry on his studies, it is a rare undergraduate who expresses spontaneous gratitude for departments of physical education, here or elsewhere. The plan and requirements of physical education usually seem to him paternalistic if not disagreeably compulsive. Perhaps most men, old as well as young, who lead moderately active physical lives, are inclined to regard their own diversions as sufficient exercise. Yet it seems surprising that in a country where the cult of athletics is as deeply rooted as it is in the United States there is no recognized cult of keeping in form. At all events, a department of physical education must find most of its moral satisfaction in doing young men good with or without show of thanks for it.

At Columbia the purpose of the physical education requirement is not principally the building up and maintenance of physical strength, but the integration of the physical life with the mental, and the development of patterns of social behavior to which the give and take of personal contact and competition, and the necessities of coordination, contribute very appreciably. We tend to forget that the young men who followed Plato and Aristotle in the groves of Academe took their physical condition quite as seriously as their learning, and gave far more time to it than do our undergraduates today.

The lessons of the war have forced a conscientious study of the credit and the debit sides of collegiate physical education; and the debit side is not reassuring—even admitting the fact that what is expected of a soldier in strength and condition is much more than the civilian may need. For us the immediate result is a thoroughly considered report from our Department of Physical Education and Hygiene (see description pp. 155 ff.). The revised program suggested by them would carry into the junior and senior years a requirement of recreational activity within a broad field of choice. In adopting this extension of the requirement, the Faculty will not be subtracting the small number of additional credits from those to be earned in other studies; for the additional credits would, under the regulations of the New York Board of Regents, have to be added to the total number of points required for graduation—an increase from 124 points to 126.

Elective Courses

WITHIN any scheme of instruction it would be difficult to state a single clear principle behind the offering or the administration of elective courses. While it is loosely assumed that there is a meeting of minds between the officers of administration and the separate departments as to what elective courses are indispensable, or contribute most to the ends of general education, the fact is that the electives in any given department are likely to reflect the department's own views of its usefulness, and to depend on the specialties (sometimes quite adventitious) which the department tends to encourage. If it happens that a Department of Biology does not offer undergraduate courses in entomology, biological education at large may not seriously suffer. Such omissions are inevitable, for highly specialized "lines" are available to undergraduates and are economically manageable only where staff and facilities are organized for the purpose. Conversely, where lines of special interest have developed over the years, time gives them status, and it would be wasteful to attempt total "coverage" for the very few students electing each subdivision of the whole.

By and large, Columbia College is exceptional, in fact highly exceptional, both for the number and the latitude of its elective courses, aided as it is by its access to the large and well-manned graduate departments of the University. For its student body of 1,800 or less, the current (1945–46) Announcement of the College, issued while we are still under the effects of war conditions, lists about 330 courses, excluding duplications—a formidable offering in itself, yet not the whole story of what is available throughout the entire University for candidates for the bachelor's degree. The content and distribution of these courses suggest both broad accomplishment and refined specialization, well conceived and well knit. If there remains something still to be done in the rebalancing of departmental electives, it must be accomplished upon the initiative of the Dean and the Committee on Instruction, and after careful study of the entire College offering. Your Committee feels that so imposing an undertaking lies outside its own powers.

There are particular things to be noted, however, with regard to particular types of courses which have developed under our general policies during the past few years, and as to which it is now possible to weigh our experience.

INTERDEPARTMENTAL COURSES

The principle of active cooperation among departments is implicit in the conduct of our introductory courses. It has been frequently extended into upperclass instruction, and it is the salient feature of our present Colloquium on Important Books. In spite of the very high usefulness of courses of this collaborative type, the staffing and administration of such courses have never been brought under any unified control, and the services of their instructors have never been adequately recognized. The root of these difficulties is that the idea of these courses has usually originated with one or a few instructors who have placed sound instruction above their expectations of reward, and they have been informally administered through the loose bargaining powers of those departments that have, so to speak, loaned these instructors to the collaborative project. There are manifest weaknesses in this situation: first of all in the absence of a secure footing for instructors who give much of their time to this sort of work. Although the departments to which these men are responsible usually lend their services ungrudgingly, and try to appraise them fairly, the services are not, in a narrower sense, rendered to the department, and the authorities in some departments have been known to neglect real claims to recognition, salary increases, and promotion.

The late Dean Hawkes considered a possible way out of this situation through the appointment of collegiate professors, or professors without departmental connections, and of teaching fellows (in the junior ranks) whose tenure and prospects would not be so dependent upon a tentative or a narrowly channeled good will. The proposal was not favorably regarded, however, by some departments, and there was the more general objection to it that it might create ambiguous responsibilities and weaken both the position of the men so appointed and their effective value to the college.

The problem of permanent organized control of such courses still remains on our hands, and it must be met, for the benefit of both instruction and instructors. A central authority should exist, perhaps a separate faculty committee, to review proposals affecting such courses, to consider the personnel of instruction, and to coordinate the interests of cooperating departments. It is doubtful whether a committee of departmental representatives could serve this purpose as well as an appointive standing committee, since the approach to these questions should be that of interest in, and knowledge of, the special situation on the part of instructors whose attitudes and influence would give assurance of competent direction.

SEMINARS, COLLOQUIUMS, AND READINGS COURSES

The view of a college classroom as a smaller lecture hall has been steadily discredited over recent years. Much of our upperclass instruction today is conducted in seminar and conference courses, a profitable method for mature and well-trained students. In such courses, as also in the relatively small number of readings courses offered to upperclassmen, there is not merely a freer understanding between instructor and student; there is an increase of responsibility for both: for the student an obligation to show resourcefulness in finding and using scholarly materials; for the instructor a relief from some of the formalities of instruction, which is probably more than offset by the necessity for a more minute scrutiny of many varieties of student work in progress.

These more liberal forms of student enterprise can be exploited still further. When a student's sincerity, capacity, and energy have been tested and disciplined in introductory courses, much can be entrusted to his interest and powers. It may well be salutary and economical for us to work steadily toward reducing "teaching" and increasing instead our criticism of the student's use of his own capacities—a workable adaptation to our purposes of the tutorial technique.

NEW AND EXPERIMENTAL FIELDS OF STUDY

Certain domains of study have been brought into academic discussion by the exigencies of warfare; the relation of these to organized peace compels consideration in any review of current educational trends.

Of these the "subject" that has been most clearly formulated in recent practice is what has come to be called "area studies."

For many years to come there will be an important demand for well-designed and well-taught courses based upon geographical areas. This demand will grow from every kind of motive, from the curiosity of the picture-viewer to the interest of the man of business with international connections, or of the student of government, economics, or international relations. At either of these extremes of motivation, the college is perhaps a less useful agency of instruction than the public lecture-platform or the graduate school. But that the college—and particularly a college with the range of opportunities that can be found within a metropolitan university—can offer serious and useful courses of this type, is self-evident.

The test of a satisfactory "area-study" course would seem

to be concentration and thoroughness. The plan of study ought not to be a mere miscellany of topical courses connected by a single geographical name. In the report of the Graduate Committee on Area Studies it was proposed that the core of instruction should be the mastery of the appropriate language, to which courses in history, economics, the sciences, or the arts, would add the successive aspects of an entire culture. But the graduate plan of work designed for students going forward to a master's degree in an exclusive field should be modified for the purposes of college juniors and seniors. The undergraduate interest in integrated "area" courses would probably come in large part from those students who do not wish to specialize in one of the traditional fields or departments, but who wish to employ their upper years in the serious exploration of a composite subject relating to a given country or part of the globe. This subject would presumably form for them the basis of a lifelong intellectual interest and possibly of a career.

Your Committee further believes that branches of study which have acquired fresh importance during the war should be enlarged and unified. Oriental and Russian studies should be variously expanded, in literature, art, economics, philosophy, and other fields of interest. Technology should also be brought as a humanistic study within reach of the student who will not be a technologist. Professor Finch, of our School of Engineering, has already plotted a course in the history of technology which should be offered in the near future.

Administering the Program

OUR system of administration is of more or less traditional type. The center of administration is naturally the Office of the Dean, who divides his responsibilities with the Associate Dean according to a pattern that is largely a matter of personal arrangement between the two officers. The standing Committee on Instruction acts for the Faculty upon questions of policy and details of procedure and control; the standing Committee on Scholarships allocates funds as its title implies, and a relatively large number of Assistants to the Dean do most of the advising of our undergraduates and keep track of their performance.

THE DEAN

It would be idle to discuss here the function of a dean. His duty can be simply stated: it is to be a good dean. And since all that we ask of him is human perfection, we can take it for granted that it is much less important to prescribe his authority and his prerogatives than to make the most of his mental and temperamental traits.

Since, however, the cabinet and the officials of the household play so important a part in the mechanism of administration, attention must be given to questions connected with these arms of authority and of academic peace.

THE COMMITTEE ON INSTRUCTION

The Dean's active right hand, except in purely office matters, is, of course, the Committee on Instruction. It has been a matter of frequent remark in recent years that the

Faculty has lost many of the functions and relations that once made it a sort of enlarged family, friendly as a group, and familiar with the common concerns and interests of all its members. Everywhere astonishing changes have taken place in faculty organization. Yet few of us who are familiar with the period thirty or forty years ago when a multitude of administrative details and questions of policy were debated earnestly at long monthly meetings of the whole faculty would feel that the newer order is without compensations.

The reasons underlying the change are easily found. First is the mere increase in the size of the College, and hence of the Faculty itself. This has greatly multiplied the number of day-to-day questions of administration and discipline with which the Faculty would under the old system be asked to deal. When our Committee on Instruction was reorganized in the early years of this century, it took over an important part of this business, and under Dean Keppel and Dean Hawkes, this device grew in importance and influence through its efficiency.

In this delegation of its powers and activities, the Faculty of the College has actually resigned itself to government by commission. But if there is general feeling that this has been more a loss than a gain, the Faculty can legislate itself out of its position as easily as it legislated itself into it. We may doubt whether many members of the Faculty have regretted this delegation of time-consuming and detailed administration to a body which through its continuity and its frequent and regular meetings is well informed in the minutiae of College business.

One criticism, however, must be noted. The Committee is composed of six Faculty members in addition to the Deans, two members being retired and replaced annually; and for many years the Faculty has voted unswervingly for the nominations brought in by the Committee on Instruction itself. In making these nominations the Committee has taken the view that the burden of work in a three-year term on this Committee should relieve any member of the Faculty of the duty of serving twice. At times the result of this policy has been that most of the senior members of the staff have been ineligible under the rule, and not infrequently the make-up of the Committee has consisted almost wholly of *juvenes imbarbati*.

Whether or not the academically unwhiskered are perfectly informed in the ways of college administration, one can urge the value of freshness and more youthful "vision," as well as the important truth that three years' membership on this Committee is in itself a valuable education in how to run a college. Until adverse judgment on this point becomes more audible, there seems little reason to argue that the Committee should show a balance of elder statesmen. If at any time the condition seems to need rectifying, there is always the possible expedient of nominations for the Committee from the floor.

There remains a more fundamental question: whether the Faculty's abandonment of direct concern with routine business has not affected the vitality, the exchange of opinions, the contacts and the intimacy which unquestionably belonged to faculties under the old tradition. Perhaps the contrast is of the same order as that between the legislative methods of a modern city and the well-known voices and personal touch of the old-fashioned New England town meeting. Size and multiplicity of functions are no encouragement to "direct" legislation.

The Dean himself has raised the question of how far the work of the Committee on Instruction should be limited to matters of instruction, and whether questions of major policy ought not to be brought before a separate Committee on Policy set up for such a purpose. Your Committee feels that any such gain might be offset by the disadvantage of multiplying committees and dividing responsibilities. The Faculty, we believe, has had no occasion within recent years to feel that important decisions have been made without a proper reference to Faculty action.

ASSISTANTS TO THE DEAN

The Assistants to the Dean are individually appointed on his nomination from among the teaching staff to assume the main burden of consultative and advisory contact with undergraduates. The group is in some degree an administrative committee without committee status and without designated collective powers. In matters calling for specific administrative action the Dean is the connecting link between this group and the Committee on Instruction.

In our system of instruction, the responsibilities of the Assistants to the Dean are of the first importance. Well-informed, sympathetic and ungrudging advice is the lubricant essential to a smooth running of the program. Advising demands an instinct for this kind of work and a lasting interest in it. Many of these officers have served in this capacity for years, on very inadequate stipends, and sometimes with a measurable sacrifice of opportunities within their own departments of instruction.

Your Committee feels very strongly that continuous, exacting, and often expert service of this sort calls for better recognition than it has so far received, and for a fairer balance between these obligations and the adviser's obligations to his own department. At present these appointments are frequently made through a gentleman's agreement with the department affected that the admitted inadequacy of salary for the service should be made up through some generally indefinite lightening of teaching obligations. But this practice inevitably distorts the effective budget of the department and creates differences of view between the individual and the department as to what, in the concrete, "relief" should amount to. If these services are taken on as "extra" remunerative work (as they generally are) they should not affect the staff member's obligation to his department—except as to adjustments during the two brief but highly congested periods of peak loads when students' programs are in the making. The remuneration for the service should be entirely adequate to the work performed and should be fully and equitably budgeted from college funds through the office of the Dean.

Moreover, it should be recognized that the demands on an adviser's time necessarily reduce his power to produce scholarly work—if he is conscientious both as an adviser and as a scholar. Consequently, it is important that his total load be kept within reasonable limits, and that rotation in the advisory service be maintained to safeguard the instructor's own professional future.

The suggestion has been made within the Committee that a large part of the advisers' work, particularly during the registration periods, is taken up with the answering of questions that are fully answered in the College Announcement and in the printed instructions to registrants: "When does Spanish B meet?" "How many points may I take in the Summer Session?" If a temporary staff of paid students were employed during the registration period to cut down these incidentals of schedule-making, the burden of the Assistants might be appreciably lessened. As it is, a notable amount of unofficial advising, by men familiar with the administrative machinery and in friendly relations with one or more students, contributes to this needed relief.

Your Committee has expressed the view that a student should normally continue with one adviser throughout his college career. At the mid-point, the upperclass adviser appointed by, and responsible to, a department or division will bring his special knowledge and interest to bear upon the maturer problems of the student. Explicit understanding through conferences between the two advisers should yield the best possible effect upon the student's plans.

GRADES AND CREDITS

Your Committee has no changes to suggest with regard to the system of grades (A, B, C, and F) now many years in use. Much has been said for and against numerical grades, letter grades, group ratings, the restriction of grades to passing and failing, and—no grades at all. If grades are accepted as a system of recording achievement, then the system we have been accustomed to seems to us as satisfactory as any other. The Committee recommends, however, that the plus and minus signs attached to letter grades should be regarded as a legal part of our system. They have been in use by many instructors for years, but have never been explicitly adopted.

What has been said with regard to the grading system your Committee affirms with regard to our recording of academic credit in points, a point being a unit of classroom work of one hour a week for one term. State boards, professional schools, and other educational institutions require interpretable values of academic work performed, and the point system in use here serves this practical purpose.

Our system of assigning maturity credits to advanced courses is only one of many devices in use throughout the country to insure a student's carrying work in the upperclasses appropriate to his maturity. It is not an attempt to rate the seriousness, the scope, the difficulty, or the serviceableness of any course; it is simply an effort to place a course where it belongs in relation to the level of a student's experience and development. The system, we believe, does not compare unfavorably with other ways of designating advanced work. Since certain acceptable programs make the total of 60 maturity credits impossible or unwise to obtain, the rule has been administered with flexibility, as all working rules should be.

THE DEGREE WITH HONORS

The conditions under which we have awarded our Bachelor's degree with honors have varied over recent years. For a decade during the 1920s we awarded honors either on departmental recommendations or on completion of special courses taken for the purpose. But except for that interval, we have followed the more usual course of American colleges and have awarded honors to students of the highest achievement, generally on the recommendations of departments and by action of the Committee on Instruction; although a student of high standing but with no clearly defined specialization might receive a degree with "General Honors."

There are patent objections to this system, even in a college of less than 2,000 students. Men of quality are not necessarily of outstanding personality; and occasions have therefore arisen in which students of very high achievement have failed to establish that achievement in the view of their department of special interest, except in the record of their grades. Those students are placed at a disadvantage to students who possess initiative and establish themselves more vividly in their instructors' minds. In the second place, there may be conflict of position and interest in the awarding of honors between a department, on the one hand, and the Committee on Instruction on the other, the department naturally feeling a sponsorship for its distinguished students and the Committee on Instruction acting for the preservation of a balance of departmental claims. In the third place, there is some ground for believing that the element of chance enters too much into the present situation, and that students exercising professional option at the end of their third year may be unwittingly underestimated a year later when honors for their class are under discussion.

In spite of these conditions there is still much diversity of opinion on the setting up of more uniform standards for Honors, and more particularly, on the question whether Honors should be awarded only to men who have declared their candidacy for the distinction, and have therefore had supervision and direction with this object in view.

A subcommittee was appointed for the study of this question. This committee was unwilling to propose a uniform plan of competition or any prescribed program for general acceptance by the departments of instruction. It was satisfied that the existing diversity was properly grounded on differences in the methods and contents of the several subjects of instruction. But the subcommittee recommends, together with a standard procedure of declared candidacy, the setting up of a Committee on Honors which shall exercise control over awards, the details of actual course and examination requirements being left, as formerly, to the departments.

ABSENCE REGULATIONS

Much difference of opinion has been voiced inside and outside the Committee as to our present regulations concerning absences from class. At present a student who counts on receiving a "B" or better in certain advanced courses can absent himself as freely as he wishes. Judgments as to the wisdom of so liberal a rule are likely to rest on the observer's view of the average student's incentives. Perhaps few among our Faculty would doubt that extremely liberal absence regulations are subject to abuse, but many of us feel that the abuse of any liberal principle is not an argument against that principle.

The fact remains, however, that the rule has occasionally

been misconstrued. As originally intended, the scheme was permissive, not mandatory upon the instructor, who retains the right to require—and to take—attendance in his course, however "advanced." Clearly, a discussion group or small reading course cannot function *in absentia,* nor can the student be said to have "passed it," in the academic sense, simply on the evidence of examinations. We assume that he must contribute to the course something that can only be contributed by his presence. Doubtless the disciplinary attitude toward absences is formalistic, but it is also true that the implied contract between teacher and student ought not to impose upon the teacher alone the obligation of incarnate presence.

Your Committee states no majority attitude upon this point, but thinks it well that the Faculty should consider afresh its individual actions under the permissive rule.

LOADING AND BALANCE OF PROGRAMS

Throughout the discussions of the Committee on Plans there have recurred practical questions connected with schedule-making. The proposals submitted to the Committee undoubtedly tend to increase the total burden of required work; to intensify the problem of program making for the first year, and perhaps, though not certainly, to make the bachelor's degree a little harder to achieve.

The general problem becomes particular in relation to (1) the proposed requirement of a 16-point two-year course in the sciences in place of the variable totals below that figure which are now possible, (2) the already effected replacement of the pre-war language requirements, which were reduced during the war, and (3) the extension of the requirement in Physical Education into both the junior and senior years.

At a glance this would seem a sizable increase. At present the aggregate point-weighting of required courses for a student taking an elementary language to meet the language requirement is 59 to 65 points (the spread being accounted for by the fact that the science and language requirements can be met through various options). For a student who can meet the language requirement by a proficiency test, without taking a language course, the required courses at present total 47 to 51 points. But with all of these proposed changes adopted, the volume of required work would go up, in points, by amounts ranging only from 1 to 2 percent, the maximum increase falling only upon students who would under the present requirement be taking the shortest possible way to the fulfillment of the science requirement.

It should be noted, moreover, that few students come to us without some competence in a foreign language; and it might be added that none should come to us without such a competence, except under rare conditions. So the maximum loading of required courses at present would probably average from about 49 points minimum to 53 points maximum. This is of course not a statistical estimate but a plausible guess. If, then, all the suggested increases were approved by the Faculty, the required courses would still average less than half the number of points necessary for graduation.

Is this an improper distribution? If we survey college practice in this respect throughout the United States we should arrive at many answers and only one generalization —of the order of the answer to the classic question, "How long should a man's legs be?" And in a way this casual comparison has a peculiar aptness, for required courses are, so to speak, the organs of academic locomotion—if they are conceived as we conceive them, that is, as enabling a student to get about in a complex intellectual world.

The objections which your Committee has heard with regard to increases in required work embrace the following considerations. (1) A program of 19 or 20 points in the freshman year, amounting to 24 or 26 hours of class work, might put a severe strain upon the men in the lowest fifth of the class, unless our admissions policy were altered to meet the change. (2) The heavy program might automatically exclude, or require exemption for, preengineering students. (3) If the sophomore year prescribed 13 or 14 points (and 17 to 19 hours of classroom work), an elective might prove a heavy additional burden. (4) A load heavy in points during the first two years might encourage premature graduation. The student who had 74 points to his credit by the end of the sophomore year might be eager to cover the remaining 50 points in a shorter time than 4 semesters. (5) Credit accounting for students transferring from other colleges with advanced standing might be disturbed, such students customarily receiving 60 points for 2 years of academic credit elsewhere, which would place them at a disadvantage with students who had completed their first 2 years of work at Columbia. (6) In general, the present list of requirements seems to fulfill the common needs of most students, and the remainder of a student's time should serve his individual needs through the provision of electives.

Discussion has elicited the following counterstatements:

(1) The method of computing points at present ought not to stand in the way of a set of requirements needed to carry out our upperclass program, and the weight of the freshman and sophomore required courses can easily be carried by our students, if we are careful to admit only those properly qualified. (2) The postponement of some required courses for students who must begin necessary work leading to specialization in the upper two years falls within the discretion of the deans and advisers. It is an administrative question whether these cases should be dealt with as exceptions, or whether the required courses in Contemporary Civilization or Humanities, for examples, might be somewhat modified for students (if they were sufficiently numerous) who were obliged to take them at a later stage and parallel to technical or other specialized courses. (3) The question of the amount of academic work that constitutes a "strain" for a student of normal capacities and sound preparation has never been really carefully examined. (4) Whether a man graduates in three and a half years or four and a half is a question that is bound to be determined by his capacity and energy. The virtue in a four-year Bachelor of Arts course is probably sentimental rather than substantial. The student should therefore be allowed to find his rate of speed in relation to a program which is at once coherent and flexible. (5) Credit for transfer students must almost necessarily be determined somewhat adversely for them in view of our special orientation courses. What is called for is simply a fair method of determining academic equivalents in courses given here and elsewhere. (6) There is (to repeat an observation already made) no simple way of reaching a

conclusion as to what proportion of a student's undergraduate work should be given to prescribed courses. The fact that confronts one in any study of American curricula is that there is a wide variety of convictions upon this point. Our practice is perhaps somewhat above the mean of contemporary practice, but the determining test should be the well-rounded preparation of the students, not an a priori view of what proportion of academic work should be expressed in stated requirements.

To these opposed views your Committee adds one consideration as to which it is unanimous: that all the problems of program-making are vastly simplified when a student enters the college with sufficient mastery of a foreign language to enable him to pass at once the language proficiency test. The Committee feels that the attainment of such proficiency should be given every encouragement in the College announcement and in a candidate's first contacts with the Committee on Admissions. It is not merely a matter of expediency for the student who comes to us with well-defined intentions; it is a sound educational principle aside from the convenience thus secured.

The Teaching Organization

THE BUDGET

Columbia College has no separate budget, though much of its work is self-contained. The problems of budgeting would be simplified if income and expense were balanced in relation to the College as a separate establishment. But the College is, fortunately, not a separate establishment. Both the College and the University at large gain from a free interchange of the services of their teaching staffs. In some cases departmental arrangements of this sort may place one school of the University under nominal debt to another. But that is primarily a bookkeeping matter which does not—as it should not—stand in the way of transfers of service within the various schools of the University.

Your Committee feels that there is no cause for anxiety in this situation. It believes, however, that the departments within the College should enjoy greater initiative in budgetary matters. This is a necessary part of greater effectiveness for the College and a better balancing of its relations with the University as a whole. If productive scholarship is more important for the graduate schools than the qualities of mind and personality that make good teachers, then the College by that very token should be the best judge of what it requires of a teacher. The connection between that initiative in judgment and the questions of appointment and promotion is self-evident. Admitting that a closed budget for the College would hamper expansion and flexibility in departmental organization, the fact remains that the interests of the College must be better expressed through budgetary policy than they have so far been.

THE DEPARTMENT AND THE DEPARTMENTAL REPRESENTATIVE

The fact that there is scarcely a department in the College which does not simultaneously draw upon the graduate staff for undergraduate teaching and contribute some of its membership to the staffing of graduate courses is, we repeat, academically sound and mutually profitable. Yet to carry out the distinct purposes of the College and of the graduate schools creates a necessary separation of management as well as organization. The reason for it is that the prime requisite of the undergraduate instructor is that he possess the personal gifts and the intellectual arts of a first-rate teacher. He should be a competent scholar, but his scholarship should be the correlative of his talent and passion for teaching. In the graduate school the instructor is first a scholar; then (generally) a teacher.

It is rare, however, that a department balances these claims with complete fairness to both sides. There are departments in which this division of obligations is explicitly recognized. The result is virtual autonomy for the College department, which initiates its own policies, follows its own administrative procedures, and maintains its own position as to appointments and promotions—always subject, of course, to the collective judgment of the department upon questions which affect its repute and its scholarly standing.

There are, on the other hand, departments in which the customary preponderance of professorial appointments in the graduate schools brings about a subordination of the College department to the department at large. In such cases the presumed *chargé d'affaires* in the College, the departmental representative, is a factotum, not an executive; policies are initiated with only a vague understanding of the needs or the ways of the College; appointments furnish a shelter for young graduates engaged in research; and in general the convenience of the department rather than the quality of collegiate instruction dictates the outline of the administrative pattern.

There is no doubt whatever that the latter type of relationship tends to destroy morale and incentive in the College teaching staff, and is a constant embarrassment to the administrative arm. The College, as has already been said, has never wished to be free from its natural attachment to the University which it has fathered, and the important link in that attachment is the over-all departmental organization. But the College must not be regarded as an outlying farm in the hands of an absentee landlord.

Even the most flexible system of over-all departmental administration must fail to meet the complex responsibilities of a College department unless the important decisions upon policy within the College are made by the members of the permanent staff attached to the College. The responsibility, moreover, for the carrying out of those decisions must be in the hands of a departmental representative who can work with freedom and initiative within his own province. Your Committee recognizes that the administrative processes of any department within the College should conform to those of the department as a whole; for there is wide variety in our forms of departmental control. But it believes that there are certain principles of administration within the College that must be kept at work for its interest, and not against it.

In the first place, the responsibilities of the departmental representative should be better defined and better understood. He is the liaison officer between his department and the College administration, but that fact tells us very little as to the area of his duties. He is not merely a clerk; that is not only the least but the worst that he can be. He is not merely the agent and interpreter of general departmental policies; he is the executive director of purposes which should originate within the College staff, which are related to the total design of the College, and which demand willing and spirited cooperation with other departments; he must be the informed judge of the teaching ability of his junior instructors; above all, he must be *persona grata* to the College administration, and must be favorably known to and respected by the College Faculty. No less than this can be asked as to the prescription of his place and his duties. But in addition to all this, he must be a personality, and as a general rule he should also be a man of rank and of mature experience.

Your Committee adds the suggestion that his responsibility and influence would be expressed more accurately if his title were changed from Departmental Representative to Chairman of the department for Columbia College. It also opens the question whether a limited tenure (long enough to be practical, short enough to allow for a turnover when the department can furnish a number of capable men to do administrative work for a limited period) might not be desirable—say three years, with the possibility of reappointment.

Your Committee feels also that action upon all questions of major policy originating in and affecting the College should be initiated by the professorial staff within the College department, subject, of course, to ratification by the University department concerned and the Dean of the College sitting with the Committee on Instruction.

To this end it recommends an annual report to be submitted to both the head of the department for the University and the Dean of the College and the Committee on Instruction, reporting the state of the College department, its plans, observations upon the teaching performance and other activities of the staff, budgetary proposals and recommendations as to appointments and promotions. Such a report might seem to impose a somewhat formal obligation upon the representative, but there can be little doubt that it could establish better understanding beween the College and its departments of instruction. And this better understanding is essential not only for the quality of instruction in the College, but for the contribution of the College to the related work of the University.

THE WORK OF THE COLLEGE IN RELATION TO THE GRADUATE SCHOOL

Much of what has been said here admits a difference between methods of undergraduate and of graduate instruction. We do not think it true, however, that the transition from the College to a graduate school implies a set of entirely different purposes pursued in entirely different ways. It has often been remarked by professors giving both graduate and undergraduate instruction that a first-rate Columbia College senior is quite as much at home in the ways of scholarship as the best candidates for the Master of Arts degree. And why should he not be, when one of the aims of our upperclass organization is to inculcate solid knowledge and habits of critical thought?

The gap between the two levels of instruction is bridged,

though not quite uniformly, by the courses numbered "100," which can be taken by both graduate and undergraduate students. Only one department, it appears, has consistently regarded it as "inconvenient" to make this concession to the intelligence and experience of our best undergraduates.

But the mere offering of a "100" course gives no assurance that the course will actually tie the threads of instruction of these two levels. Some of these courses are planned for graduate students with a remedial purpose in view. Communication is all one way and heavily informational. To a Columbia graduate coming to such courses with a developed critical outlook, and with a healthy distrust of conventional lecture methods, such courses may be, and often are, profoundly disappointing. Upon this problem an exchange of views between the undergraduate and the graduate staffs could scarcely fail to be profitable to both sides —and more important in the sequel to the students themselves, whether graduate or undergraduate.

APPOINTMENTS AND TENURE

Questions of appointment and tenure are closely knit with those affecting the interrelations of the College administration and the departments. Not uncommonly in the past, the only assurance the College has had that men appointed to its staff are the right men for its particular purpose has depended upon the soundness, the disinterestedness, and the grasp of College problems, of the graduate officers making such appointments. The office of the Dean and the Committee on Instruction have hitherto functioned only nominally in the approval or disapproval of these appointments, although the Committee on Instruction is specifically charged with responsibility for junior appointments within the College.

It is obvious that these questions should not be left to the fortunes and varieties of departmental policy nor to the equally varied individual judgments of what makes a good college teacher. The Dean himself has raised the question whether a Committee on Policy for the College might not deal more effectively with this sort of question than the Committee on Instruction. The latter committee is already burdened with administrative and regulative duties, and the policy of not reelecting a member who has served for one three-year period shelves many older or middle-aged professors of valued judgment and lasting interest in the academic scene.

If the Dean himself wishes to tap this unused reserve of knowledge and experience to strengthen his arm in the discharge of his duty, your Committee offers its hearty approval of the decision. The Committee feels, however, that such a committee, with its important advisory functions, should be the Dean's own committee, appointive, not elective; not a council made up of departmental representatives, assistants to the Dean, or any other official figures; a cabinet, in other words, and not a legislative body. If its functions were at the outset undefined, they would be at any rate elastic and informal.

Our characteristic procedure in the making of appointments is probably distinct from that of most American institutions, but not unlike that of the English and French universities. Far oftener than not, our junior instructors are promising young men from our own graduate schools, sometimes graduate students still in residence, though usually not graduates of Columbia College. Most have had teaching experience; some not. The experience of the graduate department usually furnishes a prognostic of future usefulness. And the definite lay-out of work in the elementary courses takes care of most of the problems that used to be called "supervision."

For the rest, the young instructor is obliged to rely upon his own humanity, common sense, inventiveness, and adaptability. We no longer supervise teaching through classroom inspection; we have not done so for years. Our judgments of a junior instructor's fitness for his job are derived almost wholly from personal, not official contact. The older men talk to the younger; they talk to the older men; we see them in the laboratories, or occupied with after-class conversation, or in their offices for conference; occasionally we hear echoes of student opinion, less frequently queries or complaints. Yet with all the haphazardness of these unregulated processes, we learn a great deal about a beginner's value for us; and few of us would exchange these informal and sometimes intangible evidences for the illusory proofs of competence that, up to a half-century ago, were gained from classroom visitation. Few of us, too, would think that this way of testing a new teacher is any the worse for the students, and we may add that the consideration of the student for the new instructor is today far greater than it was a generation or two back.

If a department is large, the competition of the younger

officers is lively. Only a few of them can look to permanent positions in the College or the University: there are not enough professorships to go around. We keep and promote the rare man whom we feel we must keep. The rest stay with us until offerings open up in other institutions. They have given good (and relatively inexpensive) service; we have given them marketable experience and a start in their careers. The exchange has probably been fair and profitable both ways; and with the range of choice usually open to us, we have maintained a high level of instruction, in spite of a fairly regular turnover.

Yet there are two dangers inherent in this system which have to be guarded against. The first is the tendency to academic inbreeding—the possibility of drawing too heavily upon our own schools of thought and scholarly method. The second is the temptation for the junior instructor to outstay the period of his maximum usefulness to us and ours to him.

As to the first point—academic inbreeding—it seems to be characteristic of most American colleges within universities that maintain graduate schools of high repute; and for the purposes of a university college it is probably less dangerous than it might be in other institutions. Furthermore, while a sampling of almost any large departmental staff in Columbia College would show as a rule a heavy preponderance of instructors from the graduate schools of our own university, only a small proportion of these men would be found to be graduates of Columbia College. In this respect, then, our condition is far from unhealthy, but we must be careful to keep it healthy.

As to the second point, in many of the College departments there is already a defined policy of limited tenure for instructors who cannot be promptly promoted. Yet the question remains a difficult one, for there are many human claims to be urged against a rigorous policy of limited tenure. Most of the graduate students whom we place as instructors in Columbia College are caught between two pressures; to make a decent living, and to establish their professional standing. A full-time teaching position shatters the opportunity for continuous work; so the completion of graduate work is delayed seriously, often for years. It would be easy to advise a young scholar not to marry for the time being, not to teach more than he has to, and to clear the graduate record as promptly as possible, but such advice fails to meet the real problem.

In a recent meeting of the departmental representatives for Columbia College, called mainly for the purposes of your Committee, there was practically one mind as to the advisability of limiting the period of service of instructors and assistants to about two years for assistants and three years for instructors—the period to run sequentially (that is, for five years) for assistants who are advanced to instructorships. Three or four years should be sufficient in most cases to determine whether a department could make use of an instructor on its permanent staff; in which case, although promotion might not be immediate, the continuance of the instructor's appointment should go with a clear understanding that the instructor would be promoted to the professorial staff as soon as possible. Exceptions to such a rule of limited tenure where there is no fair prospect of promotion must be few and fully explained to the appointee.

The reason for which we have most often in the past carried instructors indefinitely seems to be the very worst reason for maintaining that status—that the instructor's time has been so taken up with the obligations of teaching that he has not had the time or the reserve of mental energy to establish a scholarly place for himself, or, what is even worse, to finish his work as a graduate student. Many such instructors, placing confidence in the length and undoubted excellence of their services, build upon deferred hopes of advancement, sometimes in the face of the clearest indications that there is no such prospect; and frequently, when the separation inevitably comes about, it is with the department's knowledge that a kindness has turned out to be an unkindness.

It has also been suggested that we might add the rank of Assistant Professor to that of Instructor as grades which do not involve permanent tenure. This addition would permit capable young men to serve us longer than the statutory period here called for, would permit greater recognition, through title and salary, of distinguished service in the junior ranks, and finally would permit the holders of these Assistant Professorships to command even more readily from other institutions offers commensurate with their experience, responsibilities, and proved merits. A University committee, under the Chairmanship of Professor A. W. Thomas is now at work on these interrelated questions.

Outside the normal classified ranks there are two titles less commonly used and less clearly defined as to status: "lecturer" and "associate." A lecturer is commonly thought of as an acceptable instructor, often with another position as his vocational stand-by, who gives intermittent or partial service at the pleasure of his department and as a rule with no assurance of permanent tenure. The rank of associate was created for the College itself seven or eight years ago as a form of more or less permanent appointment for full-time instructors who were definitely not in line for promotion to assistant professorships. While appointment as an associate does not categorically exclude promotion, the probability is that it will not take place. We have appointed very few associates since the rank was created, only one of whom has been advanced to an assistant professorship.

We doubt whether the status of associate is wholly satisfactory either to the College or the appointee. It is meant to establish a status for competent men of circumscribed usefulness. But whatever satisfaction a man may take for the time being in an assurance of tenure on a level scarcely above that of instructor, in the long run the very usefulness that warranted his appointment is likely to be affected as he sees men of greater all-round value for their departments promoted over his head. It is perhaps impossible for an associate to live wholly at peace with himself under such conditions; and some departments have already felt that his service, and more particularly his spirit, seems to deteriorate under this attrition. The Committee feels very strongly that appointments to the associate rank should be made only in cases where clearly defined duties can be filled with a very certain prospect of long-term satisfaction for both parties to the understanding.

We might, on the other hand, make more use of the lecturer's rank than we have customarily done: for while "lecturer" is a title designed for a variety of special situations, for that very reason it opens up possibilities of many sorts, and particularly for a College placed at the great meeting point of the nation's intellectual and artistic activities. Probably we have always felt a little unnecessarily anxious over the difficulty of bringing the free spirit into the administrative order of the College, but certainly nowhere within the United States is there equal opportunity for wise effort in this direction.

Usage varies greatly in American colleges as to the proportion of the teaching staff holding professorial rank. In Columbia College that proportion is relatively low, reaching in some years a point only slightly above 50 percent. This may be contrasted with the more usual 60 to 80 percent at comparable institutions.

So far as this situation expresses present budgetary limitations, it can and should be corrected, but to the extent that it relates to the matter just dealt with, nothing can be done until greater uniformity has been achieved among departments with regard to the probation and promotion of junior officers of instruction. It should be added that the high percentage of instruction given in Columbia College by men below the professorial ranks does not imply any corresponding inexperience or immaturity in the staffing of our introductory courses. Preparation for the work in those courses is a tempering and maturing experience, and our men of the grade of instructor are associated with their elders in such duties (including administration and policy-making) as would qualify them for highly responsible posts in other colleges. That is in fact the basis on which they usually make the change from our midst to another institution.

THE TEACHING LOAD

The lower proportion of ranking professors in Columbia College to the total number of officers of instruction partly explains the fact that in the College a larger share of the actual costs of instruction is covered by student fees than is the case in other schools of the University. But this economy is explained in part also by the fact that the teaching load of officers of instruction in the College is probably heavier than in other divisions of the University. So many factors enter into the judgment of any man's value to the institution that it would be impossible to equalize teaching loads in mere hours of instruction; yet the fact remains that statistics on this question would show many and perhaps serious inequities in the distribution of the work of instruction—even when we take "instruction" in the widest possible sense.

Although it is perhaps impossible to initiate in the College any systematic effort to make that distribution fairer, we must record the fact that teaching obligations in Columbia College are not measured in anything like standard terms as between departments or even within a given department.

SALARIES

The question of the relation between statutory salaries and the current costs of living has been in the hands of an investigating committee appointed by the Dean. It is also, of course, a question of University policy upon which conclusive action can be taken only by the Trustees and within the limits of the University's income. So far, increases have been granted to instructors at each of the three levels within that rank. Further recommendations by the special committee are in the making.

THE FACULTY AS COMMITTEE OF THE WHOLE

We have already pointed out that within the last forty years or so the corporate role of the Faculty has undergone an important change, a change that has freed the Faculty from a large share of the routine action that once occupied the time of the periodic Faculty meetings. Today we have reached a point at which the delegation of responsibilities has made the Faculty appear at times as little more than a ratifying body; and a call for a meeting is so unexpected an event that a surprised Faculty turns immediately to its individual memorandum books to see how the disturbing event can be fitted into the framework of already posted engagements.

In some respects our size and our organization seem to be getting the best of us. One department may not know very definitely what another department is doing. It is only when questions of planning or policy become urgent, certainly not so often as once a year, that there is any free exchange of judgment upon matters affecting the whole teaching body. And the effects of the desuetude of our formal and prescribed association in the business of the College have been more marked because the large departments and divisions have tended to become socially self-sufficient, and therefore more and more cut off from general touch. We "huddle" not only in our offices, but at the Faculty Club, and we pass familiar faces on the campus or the street and wonder just where in the establishment these seemingly agreeable and interesting people belong.

It was as much in recognition of this dispersive tendency as for the actual discussion of local problems that Dean Keppel some thirty years ago introduced the "Faculty Smoker" as a sort of caucus or committee of the whole for the consideration of administrative and other questions before they were brought to the floor of a faculty meeting. Dean Hawkes used the "smoker" for the same twofold purpose, but not without awareness that it sometimes produced more smoke than fire, and with a sense of the disjunction between avowed purpose and actual contribution to policy making. The smoker gives the younger men a chance to see and to hear, to be seen and to be heard; but too frequently some of the older professors, who "have the votes," come to the following Faculty meeting innocent of a matter already thoroughly discussed, and plaintively questful of light already freely diffused. Under some other more functional name and with a sharper definition of their role, these informal meetings could easily be made to serve more satisfactorily both the administrative and the social interest of the institution.

The second of these interests is no less important than the first. The question is, how to maintain the common outlook, the ease, the amity, in a staff of a hundred and fifty-odd members, as we might expect to maintain them in a body of fifty? Or, for that matter, how to excite the fervency of conviction that could bring two white-haired old gentlemen almost to blows within the ring of Faculty seats? But if the domestic relations of our Faculty have declined with domestic relations throughout our whole civilization, there are certain respects in which the family spirit is freer and better. The relations between juniors and elder statesmen seem far closer today than when our departments were much smaller. Formerly the instructor's position was an apprenticeship. He "read" for the professor in charge of a course, gave a section in a required elementary course, and pursued a life of vaguely defined usefulness. He never carried an independent course of his own origination.

Today most of our instructors have differentiated personal responsibilities. In the "sectional" courses they plan their own work in large part; not infrequently they offer courses of their own; they participate in the discussion and the organization of departmental policies; and though they are not voting members of the faculty, they can and do contribute to the consideration of questions that affect the entire College. In that enlargement of the responsibility and influence of the junior officers there is substantial compensation for the decline in Faculty initiative.

Equipment and Facilities

THE COMMITTEE has considered a multitude of questions relating to the physical property and the teaching equipment of the College. It is an easy matter to formulate the desiderata of this part of the present survey; they can be noted simply as more space, more equipment, more—and more modern—facilities. But these questions call for thorough and detailed analysis of what we have, what we believe we need, and what can be regarded as our fair claims upon the University's resources.

The College has long since outgrown the building designed for its "home"—Hamilton Hall. This is not an old building, but it is nevertheless obsolescent for the purposes of the education we have developed. The principal problem here is simply that of usable space, particularly space for the staff offices. Although the building itself cannot of course be rebuilt, some of its most wasteful architectural features can be, with an important increase in offices and classrooms. A committee appointed by the Dean and headed by Professor Croxton has examined these possibilities very thoroughly, and its report, with architect's drawings, has been accepted by the Committee on Buildings and Grounds of the Board of Trustees.

THE LIBRARIES

From the time when it was housed in 301–312 Hamilton Hall, the Columbia College Library has always been conceived of as a collection of books especially gathered and administered for undergraduate students. The removal of the Library to South Hall did not change that conception, and the library authorities have never sought to establish in its place the practice, popular elsewhere, of a "delivery room" where textbooks and assigned readings are dealt out to students over a counter. We are all agreed that to know how to find one's way among books accessible to the hand and the eye is an integral part of the liberal education.

To encourage this attitude of self-help, the College has

for a decade maintained a Browsing Room. Recently, it has gone even further and strengthened the link between the classroom and the library by appointing the Librarian of the College Library to the teaching staff of the Contemporary Civilization course. This arrangement is designed to promote a reciprocal understanding of purposes among Faculty, students, and library. In the same spirit, most of the upper college courses have been given shelf space under proper headings in the College Library Reading Room. This permits the display not only of the books regularly assigned, but of additional volumes related to the subject. Actual experience demonstrates that this arrangement encourages initiative in study and creates a notably different and better attitude towards subject matter.

The opening of four rooms on the ground floor of South Hall for the use of the College seminars, colloquiums, and readings courses carries with it the possibility of displaying revolving collections of reference and secondary books relating to the topics discussed by the groups occupying the rooms. The College Librarian is cheerfully assuming the burden of administering this "revolving library," just as he has for some years served our educational purposes by displaying on the bulletin boards of the Library Circulation Room items clipped from periodical literature which bear upon the students' interests, or which should be brought to their notice for the widening of their interests.

MECHANICAL AND OTHER AIDS

Discussion of the provisions in the College for adequate and modern apparatus for instruction such as motion pictures, microfilm, and radio, as well as standard appliances such as charts, slides, maps, and so on, seemed to call for the appointment of another subcommittee to survey and coordinate the use of these devices. This subcommittee, under the chairmanship of Professor Zanetti, has carried on an active correspondence with all the departments of the College as to both present practice and additional needs. The findings have been included in a University-wide survey of the same problem, and appropriate action in our behalf is to be taken by the larger committee.

The Student Life

ALL THAT HAS BEEN SAID up to this point comes to rest upon the central assumption that a college exists for the purposes of the students who attend it. Its entire corporate organization and all its activities are justified or fail of justification as they meet or fail to meet its students' needs. Over the last hundred years we have come to regard the college not as a benign intellectual dictatorship, but as an intellectual republic in which standards and continuity impose the need of intelligent control, but a control exercised for the interest of its citizenry and alert to their own sense of their own needs, subject to that sense but not subjected to it. Finding the golden mean of responsible authority between paternalism and laissez faire is the perennial problem of administration, altering almost from year to year with the winds of educational method and fashion.

At Columbia, as elsewhere, the undergraduate body seems to have grown in social maturity and responsibility during recent years. Classroom disorder and horseplay on a large scale belong to the history of old and easier days, and relatively few students today think to acquire degrees by their wits rather than by work. At the same time, (or is it cause and effect?) the undergraduate is actually freer from formal and disciplinary restraints than he has ever been before. In fact his views and his influence have played no little part in that refashioning of the college system under which he has become a collaborator in, instead of a mere object for, the processes of education. Accordingly he is a more willing worker, takes initiative, lends himself to discussion, understands academic reciprocity, and finally, is in the end better educated not merely in the matter of books and the lecture room, but in the larger ways of life.

STUDENT SELF-SUPPORT

Undergraduate life is more fundamentally serious for the generality of students today because it has to be: so much larger a proportion of our students—and this is true pretty much throughout the country—are "on their own." More than half our undergraduates at Columbia are in some degree self-supporting; many of them entirely so. There are advantages and disadvantages in that. The moral advantages are frequently offset in some measure by lack of useful leisure and leisure for diversions, and there are times when hours of employment seem to have more to do with the choice of courses than does educational intent. But on the whole we can congratulate ourselves upon the fact that our undergraduates "mean business." That is a good thing for the temper and achievement of any student body.

Our serious problem in relation to the employed student

is to help him find his place as a participant in college life. If he is fully employed, he probably works during regular periods throughout the week, either afternoons or evenings. If he works in the afternoon, he studies at night; if he works in the evening, he studies in the afternoon; and that apportionment of time means that his academic day closes at noon—a serious limitation upon proper election of courses, and an effectual bar to most of the courses in science, which schedule their laboratory work for unbroken afternoon hours.

What is true of such a student's academic opportunities is equally true of his social relationships. Whatever his incentives, he is not in evidence in the hours when students with more leisure play, talk, or engage in extracurricular activities. He is generally a good citizen, but a heavily preoccupied one. We have him in probably more than normal numbers, for the metropolitan college offers openings and interests most useful from his point of view. We think sometimes that he fails to assimilate all that a diversified daylong college life might have to offer him, yet our enlarging experience over many years has told us that his presence has an inspiriting effect on the student body generally. Our task is to keep the employed student's interests in the best possible balance, to prevent his outside concerns from dominating the design of his college work, and help him as far as we can to find a congenial orbit in our social life.

SCHOLARSHIP AND FELLOWSHIP FUNDS

For many years Columbia College has had substantial resources for scholarship aid. About half is the income on endowed funds and half comes through annual appropriation from general University income. In the last normal year, total scholarship awards amounted to about $115,000, a sum roughly equal to one fifth of the income from tuition fees. Approximately 20 percent of the student body received scholarship aid in a given session.

This should be supplemented with grants of larger amount designed to cover full tuition and dormitory maintenance for students from all parts of the country. The cost of establishing ten annual regional awards (that is, with forty recipients after the third year of their establishment) would reach a maximum of either $36,000 or $40,000, depending on whether the stipends were set at $900 or $1,000 a year. Your Committee hopes that appropriations can be made to carry out these recommendations; for our expenditure upon the subsidizing of actually deserving undergraduate scholarship is below that of institutions of comparable size and importance.

Quite as urgent is the need of funds to enable graduates of Columbia College to take up graduate work without the pressure of financial need. At present the only endowed fellowship given every year to a student in any chosen field of study, and sufficient to maintain a man without dependence upon other income, is the Henry Evans Traveling Fellowship. The Kellett Fellowships, two of which are awarded annually, are for students in the humanities and for study at Oxford or Cambridge. The Proudfit Fellowship in Letters is scarcely sufficient for maintenance and is awarded only every second year. The Mitchell Fellowship is just about sufficient to cover tuition, and the Mason Fellowship in Music is not awarded regularly. The University Fellowships, while technically open to Columbia College graduates, are in fact never obtained in the first year of graduate residence, and have been so rarely given to Columbia College graduates that it seems almost a principle that they are not so awarded. Such meagre provision for aid after graduation to students of the highest merit and promise contrasts almost violently with the opportunities of this sort that are offered by other endowed institutions.

Your Committee feels that the least that could be done to encourage the proper ambitions of a graduating class of 350 men is to make available (in addition to the endowed and named fellowships already referred to) five annual awards of twelve hundred dollars each, and ten awards of three hundred dollars. The awards should be considered honors, and not merely assistance. A Committee of the Columbia College Faculty should be created to award them; and the usual provisions should be made for the return of the stipend by recipients who are able and willing to forego it.

RESIDENCE

Columbia College has always found itself in a special situation in respect to undergraduate residence. Until the removal of the college from Forty-ninth Street to Morningside Heights in 1895 there were no dormitories at all: our first dormitory, Hartley Hall, was opened in 1905. With quite adequate dormitory accommodation today, we still have a large number of students who are in fact day students, living in the city or within easy commuting distance. Like the employed students, these men often enter incompletely into the academic and extracurricular activities of the College; yet we probably would not arbitrarily alter their status if we could. It is of course necessary in the interest of our distinctive program to keep the number of such day students in reasonable proportion to the whole undergraduate body. Their influence should obviously not be allowed to limit the extent and liveliness of undergraduate life, and what is even more important, their own opportunities for social and intellectual exploration should not be confined by membership in a college of entirely local composition.

SOCIAL LIFE AND PROBLEMS

A college most of whose students reside upon its campus may not need to take pains to contrive a social life for them—though it may have to face certain difficulties to maintain a proper balance between the academic and the other activities of the student. The familiar scene—especially if it has a landscape as a backdrop, friendly proximities, sports, outdoor diversions and active fraternities—provides the soil for a natural and even lush social growth. The two questions which we have just been discussing—the employed student and the nonresident student—set different conditions for the development of our social life. Besides, the resources of the metropolis for work, for self-cultivation, or for diversion, at once expand the possibilities of a full personal life and contract the area of a generally shared social life. This is a matter for neither felicitation nor regret: it is a situation; and its actualities form the basis of our attitude with regard to the regulation of the social and moral lives of our students.

For the nonresident student, living presumably in the midst of his own elders, our responsibility in these respects is secondary, and it would be only interference to attempt to exert a ruling influence far from the limits of the campus. For the working student the problem tends to take care of itself. For the resident student we have a greater concern, but it is a concern that does not work on the presumption that the city is the natural home of the vicious or the socially deluded. There is probably no greater exposure to deleterious influences in a metropolis than in the securest retreats of the country college. We choose our students who come from distant points with an eye to the probability that they will be stable and mature enough to see and use our metropolitan advantages wisely. In the necessary regulation of the social life of resident students we establish the same liberties and the same restraints that would be found in any institution of comparable character, whether in the city or in the country. We have the temerity to believe that our undergraduates are aware of life with a more than common seriousness, and also with a more than common humor, for the precise reason that a good metropolitan college induces that kind of awareness.

DISCIPLINE AND DEMEANOR

In the domain of the intellect the student is willing, with his reservations of critical freedom, to recognize an important measure of authority in his instructors. But in his social life, his demeanor, his habits of speech, his extracurricular activities, he is likely to feel that discipline has a less clearly sanctioned function. Yet there is perhaps no other respect in which the mark of effectual college training is more unmistakable. If we cannot in four years of academic contact produce personalities at once conformable and plastic, then we have missed an important part of our opportunity to make personable and intelligent men of the world. Yet there are few periods in which this has been more difficult to do.

That problem is a grave one in almost any American college today. Democracy in education being our stated ideal, we have perforce to take on the burden of acclimating Americans of widely different background and social habits to the whole Western heritage of culture. For many students, one generation marks the step from illiteracy to cultivation. In such a rapid remaking of mental and social personality there are bound to appear residues of awkwardness, undeveloped tastes and interests, deficiencies of perception, and frequently of manners as well. These traits are offset generally by mental energy and great seriousness of purpose, but a seriousness often too intent on the business of "getting on" to a profession or to a foothold in the industrial world. It is our plain business to do our share in this work of cultural assimilation, but it is equally our duty to these very students who need it most to forestall any recoil in the process that might harm our effectiveness or our standards.

EXTRACURRICULAR INTERESTS

At their best, extracurricular activities, both athletic and nonathletic, constitute the greatest single force making for Columbia College spirit. They provide unrivaled opportunities for the development of varied talents of a nonacademic kind, yet related to intellect, character, and leadership. The division of intercollegiate athletics, which functions in close cooperation with the Department of Physical Education and Hygiene, maintained its normal activities throughout the war. But some suggestions need to be made about the nonathletic activities, which embrace the literary, dramatic, journalistic, fraternal, and other organizations.

Your Committee reaffirms the recommendations of an earlier report respecting the need of active encouragement of undergraduate effort in these voluntary organizations. The call to national service broke some happy traditions of long standing, which must now be recovered and reenforced. Those members of the Faculty who at any time past have had connections with either *The Daily Spectator, The Columbia Review,* the Debate Council, the Varsity Show, the local radio station CURC, the Van Am Society, or any of the half-dozen other undergraduate bodies, have at least a moral obligation to furnish once again that unobtrusive guidance that the students formerly relied on.

Moreover, a special study should be speedily undertaken by the Advisory Committee of King's Crown Activities, with a view to recommending action concerning the organization, financial support, and allotment of facilities to these student activities, so that they may shortly function with reasonable ease and contribute once again their share to our educational program.

With one kind of activity in especial, the language groups, even more direct action seems advisable. It would be easy to extend the familiar use of modern languages by providing language tables in the University dining rooms, and faculty participation would help to overcome the self-consciousness inseparable from beginnings: the result, we feel, would amply justify the effort.

In Conclusion

YOUR Committee stated at the outset that this report is in a very definite sense a report, not an adventure in social criticism. We have followed no devious paths of speculation. We have tried to find no changeless universal principles. We have acknowledged the sobering doubts and the flux of doctrine inherent in any great question of both philosophical and practical import. So it is neither essential nor easy to offer a final pronouncement that embodies all of Columbia's experience and collective wisdom over the years and in the present juncture.

But for the living present we have settled upon a practical view of college education in the modern world, and we have been trying to carry out that view for a generation. We want our students to know how important intellect is for the citizen of the world. The generality of men may get along without a live sense of the Copernican theory. They can live without a clear view of the nature of our social system, and they can live with no developed consciousness of books, of music, or of the plastic arts. But the man of thought cannot. He must be aware that the most trivial conveniences of his life are related to astronomical infinities, and that Thucydides pondered the same tangle of economics and politics that we do today. Our first business is to create that awareness, to post the roads of learning so that a student may recognize the continuity of the explosive present with the historical past, and may intelligently use that knowledge—within the allowances of the gods—to develop his own later usefulness and happiness.

Since the University moved to the present site fifty years ago, the College has steadily increased the value of what it has to offer. Its connection with the University is organic and of the greatest importance to students who expect before graduation to have reached the actual sources of scholarship. We have built up a carefully considered curriculum, clear in fundamental aims as well as in its recognition of the immense functional differences between the freshman and senior years. These are special achievements, which have commended themselves to serious and discerning students in every quarter of the country. We commit our future to the further proof of what has been going forward at Columbia College during the last twenty-five years.

Respectfully submitted,

H. R. Steeves, *Chairman*
Jacques Barzun, *Secretary*
Stephen F. Bayne, Jr.
Harry J. Carman
Clifford D. Carpenter
James Gutmann
Bernard O. Koopman
Nicholas McD. McKnight
Dwight C. Miner
John H. Randall, Jr.
Horace Taylor

The Program

1. Contemporary Civilization A and B

Historical. Between 1919 and 1946 the Contemporary Civilization course has been completely revised at least half a dozen times. Each revision means a rewriting of texts and a fresh selection of source readings. Here exactly is to be found the secret of the course's vitality: it has never deviated from its original principles; at the same time its work materials are constantly being tested in the light of classroom experiences and needs, as well as of a changing world which these are assumed to reflect.

The origins of the course throw light on its basic assumptions. In the midst of World War I, during 1917 and 1918, a course was established at Columbia which bore the title, "War Aims." With the end of the war, the study of "War Aims" was moved into the historical seminars and the general course in that subject was discontinued. But the members of the Faculty who had sponsored the "War Aims" course wondered if there were not some stable basis on which to organize the study of the contemporary world. They decided that an appropriate part of the curriculum of Columbia College might well be a course on "Peace Aims." The Faculty agreed; and in 1919 a course was set up bearing the title, "An Introduction to Contemporary Civilization in the West." This was to be required of all freshmen; was to meet five times a week; and was to represent a pooling of the efforts, in subject, content, and staffing, of the Departments of Economics, Government, History, and Philosophy.

In 1929, the course was expanded into a two-year program required of both freshmen and sophomores. At the present writing, the freshman classes meet four times a week and the sophomore classes three times. The four departments continue to function as a unit for the purpose of administering the two-year course. The introduction in common has enabled each department to pitch its first specialized course at a much higher level, and to assume in its special students a broad background of historical and philosophical knowledge.

The Freshman Year. The intention of the two-year requirement is a dual one: to reveal the nature of the past (both what has been rejected and what has been retained in our civilization's experiences) and to expose the insistent contemporary problems of the present which our tradition—the living past—can help us understand.

Contemporary Civilization A starts with the breakup of the Middle Ages and undertakes an analysis along three lines of inquiry which are pursued throughout. How have people made a living? How have they lived together? How have they understood the world and their relations to it? In this examination, the student meets at once two important, perhaps the most important, aspects of what has been referred to as the Western tradition: the Judaic-Christian quests for justice and love, and the Greco-Roman quests for natural law and order. Other seminal forces entered our tradition at later dates and these are closely scrutinized and evaluated when encountered historically: the growing dignity of the individual under the influence of the Renaissance and the Reformation; the revival of experimental science with its great effects on the manipulation of man's natural environment; the Enlightenment and its search for natural law in social relations; the births of democracy, liberal capitalism, and the ideal of internationalism. Through such a study of our past, values emerge: that we live in a free society in which the spirits of justice, love, and scientific inquiry have been the touchstones to social invention; that in such a society the individual has labored to achieve freedom from an arbitrary authority (whether ecclesiastical or political); and that in a climate of experimental science, technology, and liberal-capitalist institutions, man seeks to shape his world to achieve welfare for himself and for constantly growing numbers of the human race.

In the classroom these concepts are examined and tested in a great variety of ways. Take the case of the reception of Aristotle and Cicero by the Middle Ages of the twelfth and thirteenth centuries. The student reads from Aristotle and Cicero to see what meaning these had to the classical worlds. He then reads from Thomas Aquinas to comprehend what the concepts of science and natural law meant to the medieval world. Or take the case of Liberal Capitalism. The student reads, among others, from Smith, Malthus, Ricardo, Bentham, Tocqueville, and Bright. At the same time he is made to realize that the intention and institutions of liberal capitalism were undergoing a constant barrage of criticism at the hands of contemporaries. So he reads Catholic critics (Mun, Leo XIII, Pius XI); anti-libertarian critics (Carlyle, Comte); nationalist critics, (List); utopian, communist, syndicalist critics (Owen, Proudhon, Marx, Sorel, Lenin); and humanitarian critics (Kingsley, Dewey).

Techniques. The whole freshman class of some 600 students is divided into sections of from 25 to 30 men each and taught therefore in a minimum of 20 classes—and by almost as many men. That is to say, only rarely does an instructor have more than one Contemporary Civilization section—and he normally teaches it throughout the whole year. The instructors are drawn from the four participating departments—Economics, Government, History, and Philosophy—so that, in fact, each man teaches the course in terms of his own interests, training, and predilections. This is consciously encouraged; the instructor can speak with authority as a specialist at the same time that he finds it imperative to operate with intelligence in all the social sciences. The course is staffed from the College Faculty, but from time to time members from the Graduate Faculties are brought in so that fresh evaluations of content and method may be acquired.

Textbooks are being more and more subordinated as the course evolves. Originally, its main reliance was upon three texts: one in cultural and political history, one in economic history, and one in intellectual history. Since 1935 the living substance of the course has increasingly consisted of source readings, compiled by the staff, and of specialized articles, written by the staff. The framework and continuity still continue to be provided by the texts. But whenever we find a member of the staff capable of writing an illuminating and original article, he is designated to do so. Thus, to date, we possess original articles on Aristotle and St. Thomas, Mercantilism, the Scientific Revolution, the Puritan Revolution, the Enlightenment, the Labor Movements of the Nineteenth Century, a Cyclical Analysis of the English Industrial Revolution, and the like. Within the near future, under the stimulus of a new committee on revision, large additions to the original articles will be made. In time it should be possible to eliminate the textbooks entirely. The student is accordingly furnished with a manual which contains these articles, introductory notes, and additional bibliographical references.

The source readings consist of two kinds: whole documents of outstanding historical significance, and fairly long selections from books and public papers that have had a great influence on Western ideas and institutions. In the latter connection, the selections are large enough (from 10 to 100 octavo pages) to permit the student to get a clear understanding of the writer's style, his method of analysis, and the general trend of his argument.

The sourcebook and the manual are designated as follows:

Contemporary Civilization Staff of Columbia College, Columbia University, *Introduction to Contemporary Civilization in the West: a Source Book,* 2 vols., New York, Columbia University Press.

Contemporary Civilization Staff of Columbia College, Columbia University, *Introduction to Contemporary Civilization in the West: Manual,* 2 vols., Columbia University Press.

The Sophomore Year. The second year has also been undergoing a constant evolution. But its intention has always been to "raise for consideration the insistent problems of the present," viewed genetically and operationally. To amplify the background of the first year in ways appropriate to the study of "the insistent problems of the present" in the United States, the course in Contemporary Civilization B gives an account of the growth of ideas, attitudes, and institutions that are significant now in this country.

During this second year every student is further required to take at least six field trips. This supplementary work consists largely in firsthand contacts with various instruments of our industrial civilization—factories, stores, markets, and governmental institutions. These visits acquire their full meaning when discussed in the light of the explanatory and descriptive material given in the booklet *Contemporary Civilization B, Field Work Manual.*

The over-all organization of CC B embraces four general problems:

1. What have been and are to be the uses of our productive plant in achieving economic welfare?

2. How have we set about the business of governing ourselves?

3. What has been and should be the place of the United States in the world?

4. What would we, as free individuals and a free people, choose as the pattern of our society under existing conditions?

The general methodological tools employed in the analysis are again four:

1. A study of institutional formation and change in the United States.

2. Economics, with the emphasis largely on the use of our productive resources and of the things these resources create.

3. Political science, with emphasis on the organization

and functions of the American government, and on the relations of governmental units to each other.

4. History, largely concerned with the study of American social institutions and the order of events affecting our relations with other peoples.

At appropriate places in the plan of study all the methodological tools are described in theoretical terms.

The first part of CC B has this focus: the analysis is centered on an examination of the American tradition in an effort to understand what enduring values and what institutions (the ways we have devised for our guidance in living together) have come down to us out of common American experiences.

A second part, one third of the whole, also has a focus: it is an effort to understand how Americans can achieve welfare in the economic realm by the proper ordering of their economic institutions. This part of the course is clearly not an analysis of economic principles in the traditional sense. The market and price relationships must be considered, of course, but only as devices that help to explain the processes and direction of economic progress. What occurs, therefore, is a selection of basic notions—using a minimum of analytical tools and a maximum of descriptive materials—which illuminate the problem, "Is Welfare Achievable in a Free Society?"

There follows a concentration on topics selected for the elucidation of the main theme. These topics are:

1. The requirements for the maintenance of full employment. The nature of capital itself; how its formation takes

place; saving and investment; labor and its mobility; business cycles; the national product and its distribution. Monopolies and cartels, controlled prices, and government intervention. Planning: the road to serfdom or to freedom.

2. Organized labor and its rôle in connection with the achievement of welfare.

3. Money and banking. How industry is related to the functioning of our system of money and credit.

4. The United States in the world economy.

Following the study of the operation of the American economy, the concluding part of Contemporary Civilization B is devoted to a study of various phases of the functioning of the democratic process in America and of the place of the United States among the nations of the world. As in the preceding parts of the course, the approach is at the same time historical, descriptive, and analytical. In other words, the student is not merely confronted with interesting and important facts which stimulate his imagination, but is led to make intelligent use of the analytical means developed by history, government, and economics.

Moreover, the very nature of the problems studied makes it clear to him that virtually none of the insistent problems of our time can be fully understood and solved if considered in isolation from the others, or if only one aspect is singled out for special investigation. Thus, by emphasizing once more the necessity of combining the economic and political disciplines, the course acts as a convenient introduction to more advanced studies for all those who intend to major in one of the social sciences.

Among the more important topics treated in this part

of the course are the following: The Constitutional Basis of American Government; Party Government, Economic Power and Political Pressure Groups; The Democratic Control of Public Administration and the Rule of Law; The Breakdown of the International Security System of 1919; The British Empire and Its Problems, and Russia and the Western World; America's Place in the World.

Currently assigned readings are to be found in:

The Shaping of the American Tradition. Text by Louis M. Hacker; documents edited by L. M. Hacker and Helene S. Zahler. New York, Columbia University Press. (Documents ranging from William Harrison on *The State of England,* 1586, to Wendell Willkie, *One World,* 1943.)

Taylor and Associates, *Main Currents in Modern Economic Life,* Vol. I

P. M. O'Leary and J. H. Patterson, *Introduction to Money, Banking, and Corporations*

The National Resources Committee, *The Structure of the American Economy (1939)*

Robert E. Cushman, *What's Happening to Our Constitution?* Public Affairs Pamphlets No. 70, 1942

E. H. Carr, *Conditions of Peace*

E. E. Schattschneider, *Pressure Groups and Party Government*

W. I. Jennings, *The British Constitution*

P. Herring, *The Presidential Leadership*

G. Benson, *The New Centralization*

R. Pennock, *Administration and the Rule of Law*

W. T. Fox, *The Super-Powers*

N. Peffer, *America's Place in the World*

Max Laserson, *Russia and the Western World*

O. Lattimore, *Solution in Asia*

K. Boulding, *The Economics of Peace*

2. Humanities A and B

Historical. On September 23, 1937, the first class in the freshman Humanities course was held in Columbia College. To the freshmen it was merely another of the required courses which they had been asked to fit into their program; but to the teachers it was a new enterprise approached with no less enthusiasm than trepidation. The reasons for the trepidation will not be hard to understand. For one thing, the course and all its pros and cons had been discussed by the Faculty in formal and informal ways for over four years. For another, the task of teaching a collection of great books to unselected and, so to speak, unprepared freshmen, might well fill with apprehension the least self-conscious of teachers. The books themselves, more than forty in number, ranged in difficulty from the winged narrative of the *Iliad* to the forced marches of Spinoza's *Ethics*. Again, the students were being asked to read sizable portions of each book in what seemed like record time: one hundred pages of Herodotus or Rousseau overnight was a necessary but perhaps also a breakneck speed. After almost ten years of practice, there seems no reason to regret the enterprise, and there has been no reason to change its initial technique.

The course rests on a series of related assumptions: First, that a college granting the Bachelor of Arts degree should not merely pave the way to professional training, but should try to produce educated men. Second, that if educated men are those who possess an inner life of sufficient richness to withstand the slings and arrows of fortune, they must have learned to feed their souls upon good books, pictures, and music. Third, that the memorizing of labels, catchwords, and secondhand judgments about art and books is not educative in any real sense. And lastly, that to know and be at home with books a man must at some time or other read them for the first time.

The Freshman Year. In addition to taking in, however imperfectly, the message of some thirty great writers, the students in Humanities A learn one other thing of paramount educational effect. They learn that Rabelais and Montaigne and Machiavelli are readable, that they have something to say even to a scientific and sophisticated creature like the twentieth-century freshman. They become aware that these authors who have lain on library shelves anywhere from one to twenty-five centuries address themselves primarily to man as man, and only secondarily to man as philosopher, historian, or college undergraduate. No less striking to freshmen is the discovery that these men to whom they are introduced appear to have formed across time and space a kind of ideal fraternity wherein conversation and dispute, love and hate, veneration and contempt, still possess an intensity that our limited individual experience seldom affords.

These facts and assumptions concerning the humanities are what renders them in any sense teachable. Obviously the instructor cannot be at once a Greek and Latin scholar, and an expert on Shakespeare, Goethe, and all the rest. He is lucky if he has, before teaching the course, read each book half a dozen times and wandered into a few of the innumerable paths opening out from each book. But the task to be done does not require an encyclopedic scholar, or it would never get done. Nor are the freshmen expected to get what they should out of Plato, but what they can. Who indeed shall say what any man must get out of Plato? All that can safely be said of even a great scholar is that he got enough on a first reading to impel him to go back a second time.

Techniques. A few devices are employed to establish the subtle relation between information and knowledge. First, a series of short quizzes is given, each taking not more than ten minutes and preceding the several discussions devoted to each work. These quizzes are of the objective type and permit the student as well as the teacher to check up week by week on the accuracy of the reading done. Did Herodotus, for example, admire Egypt, despise Egypt, never go to Egypt, or die in Egypt? After reading 300 pages of narrative, a student should possess a residue of important facts, and in these tests the freshman class as a whole sets the minimum by the distribution of its average and extremes upon a normal curve.

The course is taught in small groups of 20 to 25 students, led by one and the same instructor throughout the year. These instructors are chosen from the departments of English, Philosophy, History, Classics, and the Modern Languages. The discussions, which employ three, four, and occasionally six class periods, permit the expression of diversified insights while reinforcing in the student's mind both the information and the wisdom derivable from each book. Four times during the year, essay examinations are given in order to test the student's power of organization and discrimination on a cumulative list of works.

From the meetings of the earliest committee in 1934 it was felt imperative to place in the students' hands the actual volumes to be read. The best of library facilities place a certain impediment in the way of absorption, and without implying any mysticism about The Poets, it is nevertheless true that some books must be read alone, in bodily comfort, and at a sitting the length of which follows desire rather than the clock. Besides, books densely packed with ideas must be marked, underlined, and annotated by the reader. Every consideration pointed to the private ownership of the books. This was in large measure achieved with the help of the Columbia University Bookstore, which agreed to sell the required volumes without profit or handling charge. The books were chosen from the three or four low-priced editions of the classics which are familiar to everyone.

FIRST SEMESTER

Homer, *Iliad* (Modern Library)

Aeschylus, *Agamemnon; Choephori; Eumenides; Prometheus Bound* (Complete Greek Drama, Random House)

Sophocles, *Oedipus, the King; Antigone; Oedipus at Colonus; Electra* (Complete Greek Drama, Random House)

Herodotus, Book I; Books VI, VII, VIII (in part) (Everyman Library)

Thucydides, Books I, II, V (in part); Books VI, VII (Modern Library)

Aristotle, *Poetics* (Oxford)

Euripides, *Electra; Trojan Women; Hippolytus; Medea* (Complete Greek Drama, Random House)

Aristophanes, *The Frogs; The Birds; The Clouds* (Complete Greek Drama, Random House)

Plato, *Apology; Symposium* (Modern Library); *Republic,* Cornford translation (Oxford)

Aristotle, *Ethics,* Books I, II, III, X (Odyssey Press)
Lucretius, *On the Nature of Things* (Everyman Library)
Vergil, *Aeneid* (Modern Library)
Bible, *The Book of Job*
Tacitus, *Annals* (in part); *Germany* (in part) (Modern Library)

Second Semester

Augustine, *Confessions* (Everyman Library)
Dante, *Inferno* (Modern Library)
Machiavelli, *The Prince* (Modern Library)
Rabelais, Books I and II (Everyman Library)
Montaigne, *Essays,* Selections, ed. by Donald Frame (Classics Club)
Shakespeare, *Macbeth; Hamlet; King Lear; Henry IV* (Parts I and II); *The Tempest* (Oxford)
Cervantes, *Don Quixote* (Part I) (Modern Library)
Milton, *Paradise Lost* (Oxford)
Spinoza, *Ethics,* Parts I, IV, V (Everyman Library)
Molière, *School for Wives; Tartuffe; Misanthrope; Physician in Spite of Himself* (Modern Library)
Swift, *Gulliver's Travels* (Modern Library)
Fielding, *Tom Jones* (Modern Library)
Rousseau, *Confessions,* Books 1, 2, 5, 6, 8, 10 (Everyman Library)
Voltaire, *Candide* (Modern Library: Part I, only)
Goethe, *Faust,* Part I (Modern Library)

One question which arose early in the discussions about the course—whether it was proper to read Aristotle or Molière or Cervantes in English—largely answered itself in practice. The knowledge of the several languages required to read all these works in their native dress would almost indefinitely postpone their enjoyment by most freshmen. The ideas they contain are complicated enough and the time available in four years of college is crowded enough to negate the counsel of perfection. The practical task was to find good translations.

Akin to the problem of securing good translations was that of deciding upon the books or parts of books that should be read. Complete satisfaction on this point is impossible. Some will want Descartes put in instead of Spinoza and would sacrifice Vergil to Chaucer. What tradition suggests, when one comes down to it, is remarkably changeful. The eighteenth century would certainly not have included Dante; the nineteenth would have frowned on Machiavelli; and the continent of Europe might even now raise questioning eyebrows at Fielding. Any list is a compromise, as is the allotment of time to each author. In both respects, we have kept our practice flexible from year to year. Nearly everyone on the staff, however, concurs in the opinion that whole books are better than parts. And where parts have to be chosen the consensus is: the longer the better.

Students and teacher accordingly feel the force of the maxim, *Ars longa, vita brevis,* but the problem tends to cause less anguish as time goes on. To be sure the dividing of his time among an introductory course in the social sciences, a course in the elements of physical science, a modern language or mathematics, and the heavy Humanities program, demands of the freshman a nicety in self-direction which can only be acquired with practice. Humanities instructors must often answer questions about the mechanics of success: Should the student read fast and sketchily or slowly and with care? Should he skip alternate assignments in his two major courses and strike an average of preparedness? Lack of counsel or of common sense makes certain freshmen neglect for a time their work in Contemporary Civilization, in the mistaken belief that 200 pages of Herodotus takes precedence—by majority rule—over twenty pages of Randall's *Making of the Modern Mind.*

Without a doubt, advice at the opening of the course on such points as these, trifling in appearance but essential to success, is a part of the proper introduction to the Humanities. But with the advice a reassuring prediction can be made, namely, that the freshman's reading speed will increase, that his grasp of ideas will grow surer, and that vocabulary, allusions, and references will become easier to catch on the wing as his stock of humanistic experience augments.

Sophomore Year. One of the original suggestions for the Humanities program provided for a two-year course which would treat examples of the several arts in chronological sequence. For a number of reasons this was deemed inadvisable and the present scheme adopted. The most important of these reasons was a technical one relating particularly to music. Music is in a sense a foreign language, only a small fraction of which can be understood without special training. Discussion about it, whether aesthetic, historical, or technical, can be of small profit to anyone unless it is preceded by the actual experience of enlightened hearing, that is, experience sufficiently vivid to establish a concept of the work under discussion in the mind of the student. Slight as the previous experience of literature and philosophy may be in the case of the average freshman, it is enormous when compared to his experience of music.

When we consider furthermore that the literature of music which is alive, that is, music which leaves the category of notes and becomes sound and therefore may be available to the non-musician as experience, is limited to a few centuries with particular emphasis on the eighteenth and nineteenth, we can understand that the study of the masterpieces of the classic or medieval periods is more appropriate to the scholar than to the average college student. An exception can be made for the Roman liturgical music which lives as a tradition of the Catholic Church service.

This limitation does not apply to the fine arts. Greek architecture and sculpture, Romanesque and Gothic architecture and painting, exist about us in original and imitative examples. The fine arts, however, which are space arts, require certain attitudes of technical observation in order to be understood intelligently, and these are akin to the requirements of sensitive hearing demanded by the time art of music. There are also elements of form, materials, and design which may profitably be studied together.

As between Humanities A and B it is equally desirable to maintain a common understanding of what is after all a common enterprise. The desideratum is not a miscellany of courses in these several "subjects," but an ordered presentation of the communicative art on its several fronts. There is no danger at Columbia that a specious unity among the arts in question will be propagated. The goal of the Humanities program from the beginning has simply been to introduce the entire undergraduate body to the several "languages" of the arts, in the belief that those arts are effective in increasing the powers and the range of the mind and that, if liberally taught, they form a logical part of any serious program of education.

Uncertainty on the part of the faculty, however, as to the strict applicability of this logic has permitted a departure from the original intention in setting up a two-year Humanities sequence. It has been made possible to substitute for Humanities B various other courses in more specific subjects in the same general field; and in fact only about a quarter of the sophomores do take Humanities B.

A recent canvassing of the faculty of Columbia College reaffirmed by a unanimous vote the original aim of the Humanities sequence. It is convinced that the Humanities B offering, in the visual arts and music, should be the normal requirement in that field, to be departed from only for good reason, and probably only by special action of the Committee on Instruction. Men intending to major in either music or the fine arts might take more intensive courses, if the department concerned judged this desirable. The Department of Music, however, proposes to substitute the new Humanities B course in music for the present Music I, offering—during the freshman year when appropriate—an advanced section for music majors and specially prepared students. The Department of Fine Arts is contemplating a similar substitution of Humanities B for its present introductory course. Students with a definite and specific program in some humanistic field—for instance, competent classical scholars working in Greek or Latin—

should of course be free to pursue that program. But the presumption remains that even such men concentrating in a special field in the Humanities should take for a full year at some time during their college career a general course of the sort next described.

Both the Departments of Fine Arts and of Music have agreed that it would be quite possible to plan their respective year courses so that students who took only the first semester would have acquired a fundamental introduction to that field. Emphasis during the required first semester of each course would be on the grammar or language of that art, developed through contact with particular masterpieces. The programs of these courses, as adopted by the two departments concerned, are as follows:

HUMANITIES B1 (Music)

1. Meets 3 hours weekly. Assignments include attendance at and reports on concerts. Sections are limited to 25 students.

2. Introductory meetings are devoted to music as a language. General principles governing tone, instruments, rhythm, melody, and harmony are explained in detail. Powers of concentration and attention in listening to music are developed in the analysis of music in the smaller forms.

3. The remaining meetings will comprise the study of a diversified selection of works from the literature of music, embracing instrumental, operatic, choral, and other vocal music, as a means of illustrating basic principles of design, style, and idiom. The student will derive from this study an understanding of the factors that contribute to unity and coherence, and a feeling for the free play of the creative imagination. He will learn to recognize types of music, polyphonic and homophonic styles, instrumental

timbre, the organizing nature of tonality, the varying treatment of thematic material, and the distinguishing features of instrumental and vocal style; he will also investigate the relationship of music, poetry, and the drama. The works to be studied will be chosen from the orchestral and chamber music of Bach, Haydn, Mozart, and Beethoven; the operas of Mozart, Wagner, and Verdi; the songs of Schubert, Schumann, and Brahms; the choral music of Bach and Handel; the keyboard music of Bach, Beethoven, Chopin, Liszt, and Brahms.

4. The student who has completed Humanities B will be adequately prepared for further study of musical style as found in the various historical epochs. The man whose studies must terminate at this point will have gained a technique of listening, some understanding of the principles of the art, and will have become familiar at least in part with a number of masterpieces of the literature.

HUMANITIES B2 (Fine Arts)

1. Meets 3 hours weekly; discussion-group method.

2. The instructor shall assume entire responsibility (within the framework of the course) for the group or groups assigned to him (not more than 25 men to a group nor more than two groups to an instructor).

3. A substantial introduction shall be devoted to the language of the visual arts, that is, to the fundamentals of design and composition in architecture, sculpture, and painting, and to the influence of materials and techniques on design in these arts. The course will next concentrate on the decorative, expressive, and illustrative possibilities of line, mass, volume, color, and texture. The students' powers of observation and responsiveness shall be progressively developed and tested by the analysis of particular works. The remaining meetings of the course shall be devoted

to an intensive study—in terms of artistic problems and content—of selected great works in each of the three major plastic arts, with the purpose of attaining the power of sensitive discernment through a constant critical attention to the qualities and meanings of the works themselves. Historical considerations, though not excluded, shall be introduced only in so far as is necessary. As many cross-contacts as possible shall be made with material presumably mastered in Humanities A and Contemporary Civilization.

4. The reading assignments shall be kept to a minimum. They shall consist of historical or interpretive works; and, in addition to the best available reproductions of the works of artists, the examination of original works in the New York area, together with outstanding publications and criticisms thereof.

5. As students acquire powers of observation and critical analysis, they shall be called upon for individual essays dealing with original works of architecture, sculpture, and painting available in the city.

3. Science A and B

Historical. The course in Science was first offered in 1934 for those Freshmen and Sophomores who were interested in science only as part of a liberal education and not as a required part of specialization in science or as a preprofessional requirement. It was given with the cooperation of all the scientific departments, in four successive sessions, separately taught. It was not practicable for the course to be given in small sections as is the case in Contemporary Civilization, nor to ask one teacher to carry the course through an entire year. Four instructors from four different departments gave the lectures, with occasional lectures by instructors representing other scientific fields. Although the four who were chiefly responsible for the instruction were from the departments of Physics, Chemistry, Geology and Zoology, respectively, constant consultations among them served to maintain the degree of unity originally aimed at. The entire course was organized around the concepts of Matter, Energy, and Radiation; the study of the earth as part of the universe; and the development of plant and animal life.

Special field trips offered an excellent opportunity to enlarge the scope of the students' experience, particularly since the College could take advantage not only of the facilities of the University itself, but also of the unequaled range of possibilities within the Metropolitan area. Within the University, visits were made to the Rutherfurd Observatory, and to the Physics Research Laboratories, where students gained an appreciation of the work of pure science on the frontiers of knowledge. Visits were also made to the

Hayden Planetarium, and (in cooperation with the course in Contemporary Civilization) a series of varied trips were offered to illustrate the application of science in industry and in the social order. Laboratory work was designed to permit the student to acquire a body of facts by direct observation in accordance with the methods and techniques of the several sciences. The readings assigned were as follows:

SCIENCE A1

Matter, Energy, and Radiation by Dunning and Paxton

SCIENCE A2

Syllabus and Laboratory Manual (prepared by the staff)
General Chemistry by H. G. Deming

SCIENCE B1

Stars and Planets by D. H. Menzel
Outlines of Geology by Longwell, Knopf, Flint, Schuchert, and Dunbar
The Earth in Space, Panorama of Physiographic Types, Physiographic Diagram of the United States, Physiographic Diagram of Europe by A. K. Lobeck (Geographical Press Publications)
Climates of the World by G. T. Trewartha (Geographical Press Publication)

SCIENCE B2

The Machinery of the Body by Carlson and Johnson
Textbook of Zoology by Curtis and Guthrie

Since the course was intended primarily for those who did not expect to specialize in any one science, but who wished to gain a reasonable understanding of the material world in which they live, it offered a wider opportunity than the standard elementary courses for an acquaintance with and understanding of the main facts, principles, and methods of modern science. Those who wished to specialize in any one science were advised to register for the strictly departmental courses in their chosen science.

With the onset of war in 1941, the course was suspended to permit the use of staff, facilities, and student effort in the emergency programs set up by the Army and Navy. Meantime, the experience gained in seven years of Science A and B suggested that the general review of the curriculum by the Committee on Plans should include a report on the Introduction to Science as a very important segment of the liberal arts offering. A subcommittee was appointed with an open mandate to recommend as it saw fit, whether resumption of the course as it stood, or minor modifications, or major changes of principle. Though working under pressure of time and duties essential to national defense, the subcommittee studied anew the educational premises and practical difficulties of an Introduction to Science, and without committing itself to a syllabus, which will take longer time to prepare, reported in favor of a reorganization of the course, as follows:

THE POTENTIAL VALUE OF THE NATURAL SCIENCES AS INSTRUMENTS OF LIBERAL EDUCATION

It is not pertinent to the aims of this report to canvass the wide variety of opinions, exhibited in current discussions of education, concerning the tasks and objectives of a liberal college. But it is not irrelevant to mention two profoundly contrasting views, explicitly or implicitly contained in some of these discussions, which have had a direct bearing on the content and practice of college instruction in the natural sciences.

One of these views, though starting nominally from the generous ideal of education as a preparation for worthy and intelligent membership in modern society, conceives the task of the liberal college in terms that are narrowly practical and vocational. According to it, a college ought to concern itself primarily with equipping students with detailed factual information and specialized skills, so that each might perform more successfully than he would otherwise the specific duties awaiting him upon graduation. College curricula ought therefore to be so planned that they will provide students preparing for a profession with the techniques and knowledge believed to be essential for a successful career in professional schools and graduate research.

The second view under discussion, while also subscribing to a no less comprehensive ideal of education as the transmission of a great cultural and intellectual heritage, in effect identifies a liberal education with familiarity with the values and the science of past ages. According to it, a college ought primarily to develop in its students a sensitivity to the ideals and modes of analysis of the founders of modern civilization, on the ground that with such an equipment students will be better prepared to understand the issues of their own age. Direct discussion of current social problems and scientific developments should therefore be kept at a minimum. For the sharp focusing of attention by immature minds on such recent matters is held to produce a parochial, controversial attitude; and in consequence, students become preoccupied with notions that have only a fleeting importance, rather than with ideas that have a perennial worth.

Both views in their practical applications represent extreme and opposing philosophies, even though the general ideals of education from which they severally take their points of departure are obviously compatible and complementary. The first view is based on the assumption that a liberal college is the place for intense specialization; and in its concern with the immediately practical it seriously underestimates the role of general ideas and general methods (as distinct from detailed factual knowledge and special techniques) in the development of a high-grade vocational and professional competence. The second view is grounded on the premise that one set of historically influential ideas has a final validity, and involves a romantic confidence in the power of what was often the best thought of previous centuries to illumine the contemporary social and scientific scene. Both views must be judged as inadequate conceptions of liberal education by anyone who is convinced that practice without principles is unenlightened and sterile, while principles without a basis in controlled inquiry are mere verbalism.

But while perhaps only a few would subscribe wholeheartedly to either of these conceptions when they are explicitly stated, they have in fact determined to a large extent the content and character of scientific instruction in secondary schools and colleges. It is worth sketching the forms under which these views have influenced science teaching in the colleges.

The prestige of natural science as an instrument in the service of industry and the needs of daily life is widespread, and its role in the recent war has certainly not diminished it. Indeed, many have come to regard the value of the natural sciences to be exhausted by their contributions to the conveniences of modern society. Science (which aims at a systematic understanding of the world) is thus easily confounded, even by well-educated men, with technology (which aims at the construction of consumers' goods on the basis of such theoretical understanding). In the eyes of many, not excluding scientific workers themselves, science is primarily a hand-maiden to the good life, a useful drudge, but hardly an integral phase of human excellence.

Moreover, it is often believed that the triumphs of modern science have been made possible only through the use of highly specialized techniques and through intense but narrow restriction of interests. Accordingly, it has been assumed that competence in the sciences, like proficiency in acrobatics, can be achieved only at the price of an early concentration upon a specialty on the part of those who are planning to devote their careers to it. Since in the light of these assumptions the sciences seem to have no bearing on the development of cultivated minds, they have often been taught either for the sake of exhibiting the gadgetry accompanying serious research, or for the sake of acquainting students with a miscellany of disconnected facts which might prove to be useful in the rounds of daily living, or to equip students with specialized skills in partial preparation for a career in pure and applied science.

The second view, that the significant content of liberal education must be stamped with finality has also left its mark upon the teaching of science. For there is an assumption widely current that the conclusions of the sciences can be communicated and understood in almost total ignorance of the methods and the logic in terms of which those conclusions are warranted. The traditional divisions of the sciences have thus been presented as the final form these disciplines must take, while the progressive overlapping of initially different types of inquiry through their use of a common set of principles has been generally ignored. Survey courses in science have been especially at fault in these respects: they have tended to present scientific findings as so many distinct items to be noted and memorized, and as conclusions for which it is inessential to advance competent evidence. Certainly, little use has been made of the opportunity in science classrooms to exhibit and develop that critical attitude toward ideas and alleged facts which the history of the sciences has actually manifested in ample measure.

Some general reflections on these preconceptions and the practices that have accompanied them are now in order.

1. The sciences have advanced not simply by a progressive accumulation of detailed facts, though such an accumulation has certainly taken place. Those advances have come about through the institution of progressively more general ideas or principles, in terms of which the available facts fall into a system or intelligible order. Doubt has sometimes been expressed whether, in the face of the cumulative increase of specialized factual information, it will be at all possible in the near future for anyone to acquire mastery over more than an insignificant sector of some

subject matter. Such melancholy doubts are not encouraged by the actual history of science. To be sure, as the frontiers of knowledge are extended, it does become more difficult for any single individual to be expertly acquainted with more than a small fraction of the factual details accumulated. Nor can it be denied that as the natural sciences extend their scope, a large number of difficult techniques must be acquired—techniques which cannot all be mastered by any single individual. Nevertheless, when a comprehensive system of principles has once been developed which is competent to cover a growing area of special fact, it is by no means essential or even useful for a scientist to acquire mastery over a miscellany of factual minutiae. On the contrary, in terms of such a pervasive system of interrelated ideas common to many distinct disciplines, it becomes easier for men working in superficially heterogeneous domains (for example, in physics as distinct from chemistry, in chemistry as contrasted with biology) to understand the special problems of these various fields and even to contribute to their resolution. The history of science thus illustrates not only a tendency to specialization, but also a significant trend toward unification on the basis of theoretical innovations and the use of general connecting ideas.

In consequence, a sound training in fundamentals of theory has been found most essential by those working on the frontiers of knowledge, whether in pure or applied science. Instruction in the sciences which emphasizes the diversity of special facts and techniques, to the exclusion of the organizing ideas through whose use our understanding of such facts and techniques is achieved and enlarged, is likely in the long run to handicap rather than advance the student preparing himself for an effective scientific career. Unless one wishes to teach science for the sake of arousing open-mouthed but empty-headed wonder over the "miracles" of science, or for the sake of developing routine technicians, emphasis on basic theory seems to be the clear order of the day.

2. Science is not only not a body of miscellaneous conclusions whose significance is exhausted by their relevance to narrowly practical matters. It is also a method of inquiry, a way of handling ideas boldly and critically, so as to yield a comprehensive understanding of nature's processes and human destiny. Viewed in the perspective of the history of culture, the natural sciences constitute an increasingly mature expression of men's desire to know the nature of things, and to achieve without illusion and in the light of such knowledge, a reasonable estimate of the conditions of human existence. Men have tried to arrive at such knowledge in many diverse ways. What is distinctive of the way of science is the logical method it employs, and the permanent criticism it exercises upon its own activity. Accordingly, one possesses only a superficial if not a distorted conception of what the conclusions of the sciences are, unless one also possesses a clear awareness of the grounds upon which those conclusions are credible, as well as some notion of the manner in which they function in the contexts of further inquiry.

In the course of its history, science has in fact made at least two essential contributions to the development of a liberal culture. It has helped to emancipate men from local prejudices and the domination of unexamined traditional beliefs, through the institution of critical methods for evaluating evidence. It has thereby fostered the sensitivity for viewing one's immediate environment in terms of fresh perspectives and alternative possibilities. The late Justice Holmes remarked that no man is civilized who has not at some time in his life questioned his first principles. Although attention to the methods of science is not the only way for attaining such a temper of mind, it is surely one of the most effective ways of doing so. And secondly, science has provided men properly trained in it with the materials for lasting intellectual and aesthetic enjoyment. For on the one hand, the systems of principles involved in the many special conclusions of science make possible an intellectual mastery over various processes of nature, and permit men to become spectators of things past and future. And on the other hand, since scientific research is an exercise in controlled imagination, and since the theoretical systems of the sciences are works of art delightful to minds trained to appreciate them, participation in the play of scientific ideas becomes an aesthetic experience of major importance.

It is these historical and potential values of the natural sciences which entitle them to an integral place in any scheme of liberal education.

GENERAL RECOMMENDATIONS

These general reflections thus bear directly on questions of educational policy. College and university education in the past has been controlled by professional ends-in-view, and indeed the early universities were established primarily for the purpose of training theologians, ministers, physicians, and lawyers. The widely acknowledged (and often criticised) undue professionalism of the modern college cannot therefore be remedied by looking to the curricula of the great universities of the past for our present models. Moreover, the sheer increase in knowledge during the past three or four centries has made it progressively more difficult to include in a college curriculum, as did schools of higher education in earlier epochs, the substance (or even a good sampling) of the contemporary information about man and his world. The pressing present problem in devising a college curriculum is to sift out from the wealth of available knowledge certain connected portions which will lend a broad significance and direction to the more specialized knowledge a man must acquire as part of his specific professional training. The problem is not that of making students familiar with material which is relevant only to a *selected* group of professional activities, even if that selected group now carries, because of historical reasons no longer pertinent, the honorific label of "the liberal professions." The problem is that of devising a curriculum which will make college students sensitive to the full range of human aspirations, which will help them to attain an intellectual poise when confronted with the various processes of nature and society, and which will develop in them a critical intelligence and a devotion to rational method in the search for knowledge.

For reasons already stated, the Science Committee believes that the natural sciences deserve an important place in a college curriculum thus conceived. It therefore recommends that a specially constructed and well-integrated two-year course in the natural sciences be a required course for all students who are candidates for a degree from Columbia College, *quite irrespective of whether such students plan to enter one of the scientific professions or not.* The Committee also believes it highly desirable that such a course be staffed by men who are prepared to give competent instruction in *all* of it, and not simply in some fragmentary portion of it. The Committee is accordingly submitting a series of tentative outlines which suggest the *sort of materials* that, in its judgment, ought to be included in such a course, though these outlines do not indicate the contemplated *organization* of the course.

The following remarks may serve to explain more fully the grounds for the Committee's general recommendation.

1. A student who does not plan to make science (whether pure or applied) his lifework, should at least be familiar with the modes of analysis in which the sciences are engaged, and with the bearing of those analyses and their conclusions upon the moral and intellectual problems of modern society. The natural sciences offer no panacea for contemporary social ills. But they illustrate in an impressive way the use of a responsible method for settling problems. Even if that method should be incapable of a simple extension and application to specifically cultural issues, ignorance of its operation should not be regarded as a prerequisite for attempted resolutions of these latter.

2. The Committee does not think it desirable to place chief stress upon the historical development of the sciences.

A course in the history of the sciences undeniably possesses great cultural and liberalizing values. But a significant understanding of the history of science can be achieved only by one who is familiar with its principles and methods; and it is the primary aim of the contemplated course to provide such competent familiarity. On the other hand, it is most desirable that a student leaving college should possess a keen sense for the fact that the sciences have not come into being ready-made, and for the fact that the latest theory in a subject (any more than a theory of an earlier vintage) is not likely to be the last one in it. It is one of the objectives set for the course as recommended to develop such a sense in students exposed to it.

3. The course as contemplated is believed by the Committee to be of fundamental value for students who are planning to train themselves for a professional career in science. To be sure, the course is not intended to equip students with specialized skills, valuable to them only as practitioners of the sciences. But the course is intended as a serious and mature introduction to the basic ideas and principles of analysis of the modern natural sciences. The Committee is of the opinion that acquisition of specialized skills, such as are involved in using expertly scientific instruments, is not essential for a thorough understanding of key ideas in science. Laboratory work, demonstrations, and the solution of definite problems will be indispensable parts of the course; but these must be instituted with a view to making explicit the scope of basic principles rather than with the aim of developing professional skills. The Committee is fully aware of the fact that in order to make himself pro-

fessionally competent, a student must at some period in his career inevitably enter upon specialization. But the Committee also believes that by developing in students a competent understanding of comprehensive principles, they will be better prepared to make a more intelligent use of special techniques and information they must eventually acquire. It is the opinion of the Committee that in the long run, and as measured by the contributions a man makes to his science, students who receive a thorough education in basic principles at the outset, compare favorably with students whose early training consists primarily in the acquisition of routine, specialized skills.

4. The success of a course in science such as is here contemplated will be seriously compromised, if such a course were required only for so-called "non-science" students. Experience has shown that the spirit and level of instruction deteriorate badly, if students are excluded from a course who, in terms of their major interests, are most likely to provide the greatest stimuli to other students and teachers alike. Nor would it be easy to attract first-class scientists, engaged either in research or in training men for their profession, into the teaching staff for a course which does not contribute to the achievement of their major objectives. Moreover, the Committee finds highly undesirable as a general educational policy, the water-tight division of students, at the very outset of their college careers, into those who are destined to go into the sciences as distinct from those who are labeled as "non-science" students. For the Committee believes that all students in Columbia College should have a genuine opportunity to contemplate seriously alternative

careers for themselves, and to make their decisions *after* rather than *before* being exposed to the materials of courses intended to make of them well-rounded individuals.

5. It seems eminently desirable to the Committee that those who will teach the contemplated course should be prepared to teach all of it. For otherwise the danger is great that the course will develop into a series of loosely connected courses, each taught by a specialist in the field who may be unfamiliar with the relevance of the ideas he is trying to communicate to other fields included in the course. One of the major values of a course planned to present as interrelated an account as is at present possible of the basic materials of the sciences would then be forfeited.

6. For reasons that will presently be mentioned, the Committee is not submitting any adequately worked-out plan for an integrated science course, and the outlines which form part of this report do not convey satisfactorily the conception of such a course with which the Committee has been working. Indeed, to the casual reader those outlines might suggest what is certainly not the case, that all the Committee has in mind is a slight refurbishing of standard courses in the sciences. On the other hand, the Committee wishes to make clear that it is not recommending the abolition of the traditional divisions between the various natural sciences, and is not aiming to place upon the Procrustean bed of a few general principles the vast array of materials contained in the physical and biological disciplines. The Committee does not think that an artificial integration of the sciences is worth while, or that a more unified account of basic scientific materials is possible than is at present

exhibited by those materials. What the Committee does maintain is that different sciences share common principles of explanation to a greater extent than superficially appears or is commonly believed, and that it is essential for sound instruction in the sciences to make such principles explicit and their relevance to different fields plain. As a small indication of what the Committee has in mind, it should be noted that no special outline has been submitted for geology. This is a consequence neither of neglect nor of a conviction that geology has no place in a scheme of liberal education. It is a consequence of the assumption that certain important materials of geology can be more profitably presented and studied *in connection with other themes*, rather than in isolation: some parts of geology in connection with astronomy, some in relation to biology, and some in connection with the materials surveyed in the course on Contemporary Civilization. It is some such reorganization of the basic materials of the sciences that the Committee has in mind.

ADMINISTRATIVE AND STAFF PROBLEMS

Although the Committee has not been directed to consider the various administrative problems involved in instituting a new course in science for lower classmen, it has not been able to avoid giving some attention to a few of them. But in any event, since the realization of the Committee's plans is contingent on finding a solution to them, these problems must be frankly faced.

1. A substantial majority of students now entering Columbia College wish to prepare themselves for some profes-

sional schools. In order to meet the entrance requirements of such schools (and also of graduate schools in the sciences), those students must satisfactorily complete a considerable number of fairly specialized science courses —courses whose contents inevitably overlap with the materials of the course as planned by this Committee. The question naturally arises how such students, if they are compelled to take this latter course, will find the time to satisfy the requirements of the professional and graduate schools. The obvious way out seems to be to exempt pre-professional students from the unified science course, provided that they substitute for it some series of standard courses demanded by the professional schools they are planning to enter. The Science Committee is unalterably opposed to such a compromise with its ideals.

On the other hand, the Committee is not prepared to suggest how this serious difficulty may be overcome. It is conceivable that professional schools may be persuaded to accept the unified course, as at least a partial substitute for their present requirements. It is also possible that in the interest of maintaining a liberal college, Columbia College may deliberately discourage admitting students concerned primarily with meeting pre-professional requirements—though the adoption of such a policy certainly raises budgetary problems of considerable magnitude.

It should be mentioned, however, that in the opinion of the Committee, courses now offered by various science departments in the University often duplicate one another at least in part, and that more time could be won by pre-professional students for such a course as the Committee is contemplating by revising (in some cases to a not inconsiderable degree, it must be admitted) the present schedule of offerings. But such a revision is clearly contingent upon the development of an enthusiastic support by the various science departments of the University of the Committee's plans for a unified course in science.

2. The problem of staffing and financing a course such as is here contemplated is a serious one. The Committee assumes that the course would be given in small sections of not more than 25 students each, and that therefore a teaching staff of something like 20 men will be required. It is also clear that additional laboratory facilities must be found if the course is to be properly conducted.

Moreover, if the Committee's recommendation be accepted, according to which those teaching the course must be qualified to give instruction in the whole of it, the teaching staff for it must consist of highly mature and unusually well-equipped men. The Committee has given some thought to the question of how such a select group of men is to be found. It believes that such a group can be slowly developed at the University through the continued association, over a period of years, of men interested in participating in the course—in effect, through the establishment of a sort of colloquium in which specialists in different branches of science would help each other to acquire a competent knowledge of fields other than their own.

However, the realization of such a scheme precludes a large turnover in the staff teaching this course. It also precludes using graduate students and recent recipients of the doctor's degree as temporary instructors. No course is better than the man who teaches it, however attractive it may appear on paper. If the course in science is to be of genuine worth, its teachers must be selected from those members of the College and University staffs who can afford time from research for first-class teaching in the College, and who can look forward securely to years of steady personal development in their association with the course.

APOLOGIA AND FINAL REMARKS

The Science Committee is unable to submit at this time a carefully worked-out syllabus for the course described in general terms. It is only proper to offer some words of explanation.

1. The Committee has been meeting during years when the best efforts of scientists have been directed to other ends than either theoretical research or teaching. It has therefore not been able to obtain the advice or the full cooperation of men whose judgments and aid it would have most desired to receive. In addition, and for the same reason, the Committee has not had a physicist taking active part in its deliberations; it has had the advice of its mathematical member for only a few months; and a large proportion of its other members have been able to afford only the minimum amount of time and effort to the work of the Committee. Under the circumstances it has been physically impossible to complete the task assigned to the Committee.

2. Although the Committee has succeeded in formulating a few general principles and a number of tentative outlines of the materials to be included in the course, it believes that both principles and outlines require further study and

discussion before they can be taken as the basis for constructing a detailed syllabus. The advice of men recently returned to the campus from war duties must be obtained, and the feasibility of such a course as is here contemplated must be carefully investigated through consultation with the various science departments.

3. The construction of a detailed syllabus will require much time and effort. Members of the Committee are therefore unwilling to undertake the actual task of construction, unless they obtain some expression from the Faculty that the general ideas underlying this report are acceptable to it, and unless they are given some assurance that such a syllabus would become the basis (in substance if not in details) for a science course for lower classmen in Columbia College.

The Committee therefore specifically recommends that the general proposals herein contained be submitted to the Faculty for its judgment. It further recommends that should the Faculty act favorably on this report, a new Science Committee of not less than three men be appointed to construct a detailed syllabus of instruction, the members of such a committee being relieved of all other College and University duties during the period of their membership.

TENTATIVE OUTLINES FOR THE COURSE IN SCIENCE

The Committee's idea of an integrated course in science will perhaps be more clearly understood if a brief sketch is first drawn of the materials and their organization.

The range of the course extends from the principles underlying the behavior of gross and microscopic bodies to the nature and activities of living organisms. Since the understanding of biological phenomena depends in many cases on a firm grasp of physical and chemical laws, these latter constitute the initial subject of study. But whenever and wherever it is pedagogically advisable to do so, the principles dealing primarily with inanimate nature will be illustrated by biological phenomena as well.

At the same time, it should be pointed out that though all the sciences may be developed in a continuous manner from electrons and protons to complex populations of biological individuals, the sciences themselves have not developed in this way. This fact of history is given appropriate pedagogical recognition. The Committee is thus entirely clear on the issue that different portions of the sciences can be developed and presented autonomously; and accordingly, many of the topics discussed are expounded as parts of a self-contained discipline.

The course begins with an investigation of the physics of macroscopic phenomena, the inquiry taking its point of departure from the behavior of celestial bodies as illustrative of fundamental principles of mechanics. In this connection, the introductory ideas of the mathematical theory of limits are presented, special attention being given to such notions as velocity and area as examples of derivatives and integrals, respectively. The kinetic theory of matter is studied next, and its scope and power are developed in terms of the properties of gases, liquids, and solids.

With the introduction of the basic ideas and laws of electromagnetic phenomena, the physics of particles is then temporarily abandoned, so that the student is gradually made familiar with the concepts of field physics, and with the fundamental interconnections between electricity and optics. The discussion of particle physics is then once more resumed with the study of the structure of atoms and molecules; and following this road, the student is introduced to the Periodic Table of the elements and the Bohr model of the atom. The basic ideas of the special theory of relativity are next studied, prefaced by a discussion of alternative geometric systems and of the axiomatic method. The student will now be prepared to consider certain cosmological questions, such as the composition of the sun and the stars and the age of the universe.

The fundamental notions of chemical analysis and the main types of chemical reactions are next introduced, the specific materials investigated being systematically explained in terms of the structures of atoms and molecules elaborated earlier in the course. The concept of equilibrium, which forms the next subject of study, provides the opportunity for developing elementary concepts of probability and extending these ideas into a discussion of equilibrium between states of matter, between molecules in chemical reactions, and between ions and electrons. With an introduction to the chemistry of carbon, the student is brought to the traditional boundary between the physico-chemical and the biological sciences—though, as already noted, the relevance of physical and chemical knowledge for the understanding of living matter will be consistently emphasized in the preceding studies.

The structure and function of biological individuals are next investigated, and their continued maintenance as biochemical systems is examined; this portion of the course is devoted to the study of such phenomena as photosynthesis, the processes of oxidation and reduction, respiration, the operations of the carbon and nitrogen cycles, and the functions of the sense organs and the nervous system. Problems relating to the origin and development of biological individuals and species are next explored, so that the student will become familiar with the fundamental laws of biological inheritance, the interrelations of various forms of organic life, and the nature and conditions of processes of growth.

The course terminates with brief but systematic reflections on the methods with the aid of which the wide range of conclusions previously studied have been achieved and tested. This involves the study of formal logic and probability, and such allied mathematical questions as counting, measurement, and infinity.

4. Foreign Languages

Historical. In the twenty-five years between the two world wars, foreign language study in the American colleges was under heavy pressure. The time of the students had been progressively preempted by course requirements of a general educational character imposed in the freshman and sophomore years and by the increasing intensity of preprofessional demands throughout the undergraduate period. The consequent undermining of language study was accelerated by the attitude of preprofessional advisers, some of whom take the position that the foreign languages have only a "tool value" for usefulness in social and scientific pursuits, a thesis which disregards the history of liberal studies since the Renaissance.

Techniques. Under this theory it was thought safe to reduce foreign language study to the minimum needed to provide a tool for opening the way to more important subject matter in other fields, and this view was acted upon in Columbia College by substituting a test of reading ability for the traditional course-requirements in the foreign languages. This action, logical enough if one accepts the premises, ignored fundamental aspects of the contribution which courses of instruction in the foreign languages make toward a liberal education. It failed to recognize the vital relationship between language and all other forms of humanistic culture, or the liberalizing influence of contact with the foreign civilization under the leadership of a scholarly teacher, whether the classics or current literature be used.

Columbia College is by no means the only institution where work in foreign languages has deteriorated in the past two decades, although the older institutions in the East do not appear to have followed its lead in substituting a reading test for college courses. On the other hand, the pressure of new courses on the curriculum, particularly courses in the social sciences, has already cut so deeply into the time allotted to foreign language study that twenty years ago a Committee of the American Council on Education reported that language teachers would have to concentrate on *one* objective if they were to assure their students of any surrender value after formal study ceased, and that since ability to read the language with fluency was the foremost need, and indeed, the only need for the great majority of American citizens, teachers should make reading ability their first goal.

In fulfillment of this requirement they recommended a more purposeful organization of time and materials of instruction. This has been realized in great part by the construction of frequency word-books and idiom lists in the main languages, and the creation of standardized tests. This realistic approach has undoubtedly had a beneficial effect on the two-year course: in the past decade scarcely one instruction book or reading text in French, German, or Spanish has been published in this country without use of the frequency studies referred to, and the employment of standardized tests to measure progress has become general in the better schools and colleges. Those who reproduce the dusty old caricature of the foreign language teacher as a dealer in subtle grammatical distinctions and a digger of etymological roots are quite ignorant of the immense effort that this group of teachers has made in the past fifteen years to standardize and rationalize teaching and testing materials in order to accelerate the process of learning the foreign languages for practical usefulness with the greatest economy of time. No subject in the curriculum has engaged the combined effort of psychologists and subject-matter teachers so actively in research and experiment.

Lessons from the Army Specialized Training Program. Nevertheless, for the great majority of students, curricular conditions have tended to limit achievement to reading ability. The lessened emphasis on oral training entailed a loss in the interest of students, who find a real stimulus in learning to use the language orally. This was very evident when the Army put its Specialized Training Program into effect in 1943 and set oral competence as the prime objective. Many thousands of soldier-students, with widely varying preparation, were assigned for training in the modern foreign languages, which extended over three twelve-week terms, with fifteen hours per week of class and group instruction and practice. Two thirds of this time was allotted for practice in groups of ten or less, under the leadership of a native or bilingual instructor. In February–March, 1944, a Committee of the Modern Language Association of America visited a large number of the colleges where this work was in progress. Their report, based on visits to 427 classes distributed from Massachusetts to Iowa and Kentucky, and on interviews with more than 1,000 officers, instructors, and students, declares that the following results were ascertained:

The student is able to understand the languages as spoken by a native on a considerable range of subjects.
He is able to speak intelligibly on a considerable range of subjects.
He is able to write the Western European languages.
He is able to read the languages with astonishing facility.

Even if this report be too roseate, there is abundant evidence that the Army courses have shown that the young American can master a foreign language for practical use if he is able to devote himself to it intensively. A great variety of practices were encountered by the visitors of the M.L.A., but in cases where the Army requirements were adapted intelligently, success was noteworthy. Of great importance were supplementary aids to learning, such as phonographic records, moving pictures, radio, and social contacts in language houses and clubs and with foreign groups. In general, success was due to the following factors, in addition to very careful organization of materials and the enlistment of experienced teachers, under centralized supervision:

Increased number of hours in contact with instructor;
Small groups with native or bilingual drilling;
Career motivation—military future;
Stimulation of student interest through simultaneous study of foreign areas.

New Orientation in Foreign Language Teaching. The success of the Army Program has kindled a lively interest in foreign language study in a number of the institutions, and many qualified observers believe that foreign language study is about to enter on a fresh period of development, with a new motivation and new objectives. A number of colleges are preparing to revise the curriculum in order to provide opportunity for intensive study, and several deans have shown their willingness to make budgetary increases for that purpose.

Columbia College will certainly not be the last to undertake an intensive course in foreign languages to meet the needs of the post-war period. Obviously it should not introduce revolutionary changes until it is assured that these will bring results corresponding to the outlay in time and money. Whatever program it undertakes should be aimed to serve more adequately the two main purposes of foreign language teaching in an American college: the humanizing influence of literary study and the practical advantage of direct contact with the thought and culture of a foreign people.

Accordingly, Columbia College will offer, beginning in 1946–1947, an intensive elementary course of ten hours per week, five hours to be devoted to oral practice in small groups under a bilingual or foreign instructor. The course will be optional and an alternative to the traditional five-hour elementary courses, which are to continue, at least for the present. If this experiment is successful, the double expenditure of time will receive its compensation through a saving in the succeeding year, inasmuch as the attainment of the academic goal—passing the Proficiency Test—should be accomplished in one year instead of the two years necessary in the traditional course.

We propose to retain the Proficiency Test, but to add a test in understanding the spoken language and in speaking it. It is not clear how far oral drill is of aid in learning to read a language, but those who observed the Army courses believe that it is of important help. It is our opinion that in the development of language competence the two skills, reading ability and oral proficiency, are mutually helpful, and that for Columbia graduates, many of whom will have a part in the closer international contacts of coming decades, the ability to speak a foreign language with even a moderate degree of fluency will be an asset of great importance. We are well aware that this ability deteriorates rapidly unless practiced, but it is our expectation that those students who attain it *early* in the college career will feel the urge to maintain it thereafter.

Here follows in brief outline the new program of intensive elementary, expanded intermediate, and advanced work in foreign languages available to undergraduates beginning in 1946–1947:

Elementary: Regular Course, A1–A2, five hours per week, 4 points. Grammar, introduction to reading, oral practice.

Intensive Course, 1–2, ten hours per week, 6 points. (a) Grammar and reading section, five hours per week, 4 points; sections limited to 25 students. Grammatical analysis, vocabulary training, reading practice, with full preparation. (b) Drill sections, five hours per week, 2 points; groups limited to ten. Oral exercises, based on handbook and realia; student dialogues, reports, etc. All work of groups in foreign language. Little or no outside preparation.

Intermediate (to follow A1–A2, not the 1–2 Intensive Course): B1–B2—Grammar and reading course, four hours per week, 4 points; sections limited to 25 students. Grammatical review; intensive and extensive reading for vocabulary building and cultivation of reading readiness at sight, with full preparation.

BO1–BO2—Oral and aural drill, two hours per week, 2 points. Sections limited to 12 students. All exercises to be in the foreign language, including student-dialogues, reports on outside reading, dictation, etc.; with preparation by linguaphone practice and rehearsal of conversational material.

PLACEMENT TEST: The placement test in foreign languages should include a test on the aural understanding of the languages, to be given by the department concerned.

PROFICIENCY TEST: The test should consist of two parts: (1) Test in reading the language, as heretofore, with strict interpretation of the requirements as defined by the College Faculty. (2) Test in oral and aural proficiency, as defined by the Language Committee based on the first year of experience with the new program.

The revised Proficiency Test should go into effect at the end of the first year under the new program.

ADVANCED COURSES: Courses above the B grade should be such as the departments have found most practical for further training in the languages and for guidance in the study of the literary and other culture of the foreign people. So far as possible they should be conducted in the foreign language, and readings assigned in that language. It is felt that each of the following types of course should be included in the departmental offering, at least in alternate years: (1) A course in language usage for development of greater proficiency and correctness in speaking and writing. (2) A course in one or more of the greatest authors in the language under study. (3) A course in the traditional and contemporary culture of the foreign people, including, so far as possible, the following aspects: geographical situation, political and social institutions, art, education, and other phases of humanistic culture.

5. English Composition

Historical. The root of almost all student failures in the adequate use of our language is what seems to us a long-standing error—the separation almost a century ago of instruction in writing in the American colleges from the general instruction. This separation was perhaps an economy and a convenience, but its effect over the years has been to place all responsibility for sound writing upon a single department, which by the very acceptance of that responsibility lost its power to enforce its discipline upon the written work of any and every other field. The traditional training in command of one's own language as the vehicle of all communication and discussion was replaced by the "teaching" of the language as a "subject," generally with a false and usually unrealized literary aim. The final consequence has been the all but complete disregard of a student's written performance in any courses but those in composition, on the specious ground that his responsibility in other courses was only for "matter," and that the instructor's criticism of writing as writing was an unnecessary if not intrusive niceness.

That is the briefest possible statement of the present situation as to instruction and practice in the use of the language. Its truth would be conceded by any good college in any quarter of the United States. At best, and at any time in its history, the separation of composition from general instruction has never worked. Its gravest defects were only partially apparent, however, so long as secondary school programs gave adequate attention and time to training in elementals—say, down to the first quarter of our century. Since that time the situation has become desperately grave.

Not many years ago practically every major Eastern college required of its entering freshman a written examination in English, generally the approved examination of the College Entrance Examination Board. The quality of the writing on this examination was an essential and carefully judged criterion for entrance. The examinations were competently read, and every college that used them could feel confidence in their results and base its formal work in composition upon the assumption that the members of its freshman class "could write."

As a matter of history, this almost complete dependence upon the Board and its standards gradually broke down; first of all, perhaps, because of the view that the Board examinations favored candidates for entrance to college who had gone through the specialized and generally expensive training of the private preparatory schools. With the enormous increase in the number of high school students after 1900, the colleges themselves began to adopt policies that removed for qualified high school students most of the disadvantages of such competition. The way was generally simple—a change-over from a standardized examination system to the use of the high school record itself as the most important evidence of an applicant's fitness to undertake college work. Viewed fairly, the change in policy was an entirely proper one in a patently changing situation, but there were accompaniments to the change that were not wholly healthful for the colleges; for from the beginning it was clear that the highly variable standards of high schools all over the nation provided less reliable judgments and greater academic risks in the admission of freshmen. There is no subject in which this has been more seriously evident than in English.

Unhappily, this change in entrance procedures came during the same period in which, for various reasons, the "subject" of English, and particularly composition, took more and more battering from educational reformers, educational politicians, and, most of all, unqualified teachers who had swarmed into the places created for them by a furiously expanding high school system. Reasonable proficiency in writing, which had been the backbone of the preparatory school system, as it has been in every system of sound education, gave way before "practical considerations," negligence, and sometimes contempt. In both rural and urban high schools there was the feeling that the needs of the minority of students with aspirations must not interfere with those whose high school work was the final stage of their education, and who were "preparing for life." "Essentials," therefore, could not be sacrificed for the graces; and writing one's own language literately and clearly was not considered an essential. The problems of congested classrooms, of the "melting-pot" for the children of immigrants, of poorly equipped teachers who knew more about pedagogical principles than about their subject, of teaching loads that made attentive theme-reading almost an impossibility, all contributed to a neglect that was first defended, then standardized, and not infrequently rationalized in the name of progressive education.

Sound instruction in composition on the elementary and secondary levels has always been a painstaking and time-consuming process, both for teacher and student. But it is something that can be done. It is one thing that the private preparatory school did accomplish consistently and over the years. But today the fact can be summarily stated, and without qualification, that the writing of a very large proportion of our American high school graduates is bad writing. It is bad even for the everyday purposes of life, and particularly bad, sometimes incredibly bad, for what must be expected from a man in college.

The expedient which the English Department has to adopt to raise gross ineptitude to a level at which our freshman course in English can be intelligently taken is a remedial elementary course (without academic credit) on a level below the maturity of a well-administered tenth-year course in high school. But such a course can be given, and it can save from academic perdition half the men who are obliged to take it. The other half includes many men so undernourished mentally that their chances of reaching the end of the sophomore year are very doubtful. There is a suggestive correlation between students of this very low level of accomplishment in English and those who drop out of the College fairly promptly because of mental inertia or general incompetence.

But this remedial course meets only the very worst of the problem. The distressing mediocrity of the writing of probably half our freshmen has to be worked with in our required course in composition, which is designed to meet the needs of men of some maturity and training. An English Department can deal only with the symptoms of this low intellectual health. The organic difficulty it cannot adequately prescribe for, because the problems of expression are a function of every part of, and every subject in, the general education, and for years we have failed or refused to recognize this plain fact.

Instruction in composition in Columbia College has had its ups and downs, but at best it has been, as it is for almost every American college, a *pis aller*—the best that can be done with a bad situation. This has been more notably true in Columbia College since the introduction of the Humanities course; for the setting up of Humanities A as a required course all but eliminated the traditional freshman requirement in English. Since 1938 this requirement, and therefore the time spent upon it by the student, has been quantitatively negligible, except in cases of sheer incompetence.

Techniques. This glance at the history of our problem is enough to make it clear that now more than ever we must reassert the principle that the writing of one's language is inseparable from our entire plan of instruction, and that we must as promptly as possible take the first steps to reestablish its indispensableness and its dignity throughout all our educational undertakings. But the rehabilitation of such instruction will take time and effort. There is inertia to be overcome—the objection of many instructors that it will require time better spent on the "matter" of a course; unfamiliar procedure; positive resistance to the spending of effort upon what some instructors may perhaps feel to be outside their proper sphere.

With these facts before it, the Department of English decided to present its case, first of all, to the teaching staffs of freshman courses in Contemporary Civilization and Humanities, as a group who could recognize the problem at its lowest point of incidence, who would be least likely to be affected by any aversion to direct and serious concern with the question, and whose influence, brought to bear upon students from their first day of residence in the College, would be immediate and decisive. If these two groups could be persuaded to accept the principle we have stated, and to lend their support to its realization, the College would have taken an important first step toward the improvement of the situation. Without their approval and support, it would seem idle to anticipate effective support from instructors remoter in interest or less affected by the problem.

The Contemporary Civilization and Humanities staffs brought to this discussion vigorous interest, and approved without a dissenting voice these propositions: (1) that quality of written performance should be a recognized part of the standards of these two courses, (2) that greater opportunity should be provided for written work in these courses, and that this written work should be judged and criticized as writing, (3) that the staffs of the two courses would undertake to put these views and procedures into immediate effect during the present term, and would act in cooperation with the English Department to further these ends, and (4) that the underlying principle should finally be approved and established by vote of the faculty with respect to all courses given in Columbia College.

It is not proposed, nor is it possible, to transfer to the

Contemporary Civilization and Humanities courses the burden of formal instruction in the use of the language. That is obviously the work of a Department organized for the purpose. The collaborating instructors can give their moral support to a practicable standard and hold their students to requirements of clarity, logical connection, the use of the right word and the right phrase, and, in general, economy, directness, unpretentiousness, and sincerity of expression. If these instructors have time and will to deal with the hundred errors in grammar, syntax, punctuation, and the like which deficient high school preparation has failed to eradicate, so much the better. But the essential object of this joint effort is to convince the student that competent writing is competent writing, always and everywhere, and not the isolated concern of any one department.

Additional Freshman Work in English Composition. So long as the preparation of entering students is what it is today, the English Department must carry on organized instruction in English adjusted to individual needs. This means, for the ill-prepared, a required elementary course without academic credit, to be followed by the customary freshman course when the student is prepared to take it with understanding and advantage. The regular freshman course should be properly meshed with the Contemporary Civilization and Humanities courses by bringing it entirely within the freshman year (at present it is spread over the freshman and sophomore years). This course, given two hours a week, but counting as one point each term, will be weighted with exactly the hours and credits now given in

English C. The course will call for a minimum of outside preparation. Students whose ability to write is clearly established on an entrance examination should be exempt from it. But any exempt student whose writing in either Humanities or Contemporary Civilization is seriously and persistently faulty should be recommitted to the required course in freshman English.

The Department of English is unanimously of the opinion that no student should be admitted to Columbia College who has not taken an acceptable examination in English *before his admission,* that examination to be used as an important criterion of eligibility. The Department urges this not because it would clear the way for effective instruction in the freshman year (though that fact has its importance), but because a written examination in English is, in all informed opinion, one of the most useful evidences of capacity to carry on college work, particularly if it is read diagnostically and the results in doubtful cases reported in terms which can aid in the assembling of a competent judgment of the applicant's general fitness. The College Entrance Board tests have over many years, because of high standardization and accurate reporting, served this purpose better than any other examinations. But it would no doubt be necessary for the College itself to give examinations for students who had not taken Board examinations. Substitutes for these examinations, such as high school or state board examinations, the Department looks upon with the greatest skepticism, as to standards, controls, and methods of grading. They are no adequate test of the things we want to know.

It is not invariably necessary, perhaps, that an applicant should "pass" such an entrance examination in English, for there are sometimes reasons, generally discernible to a qualified reader, for inability to quite make the grade. But the examination should certainly be taken by everyone of our applicants, for without it we are without the single most pertinent item of information as to a student's power to use his mind as the College must expect him to use it.

If these recommendations can be realized, this Department is confident that the quality of our students' written work can be brought to a satisfactory level of effectiveness. The process will take time and unswerving attention, for there are great and long-standing difficulties to be met. But with the reestablishment of the use of the language as a comprehensive discipline, which should not be and cannot be sidestepped by either instructor or student, we have at least laid down a norm under which we can work seriously and intelligently.

6. Physical Education and Hygiene

Historical. Columbia College was one of the first American colleges to require physical education for all freshmen and sophomore students: ". . . . as a part of the new curriculum physical education is prescribed for all first and second year students." (Minutes of the Meeting of the Faculty of Columbia College, 1897.) The same two-year requirement continued without change until the current war program was inaugurated. During the school year 1942–43 the Faculty of Columbia College adopted an extension of the two-year prescription to include juniors and seniors. However, the requirement was not enforced, and owing to the well-nigh complete elimination of the upper College through enlistments, it was dropped the following year. In July, 1943, when Navy V–12 students were admitted to Columbia, an additional modification of the program was made to comply with the Navy V–12 curriculum. In accordance with these Navy regulations, V–12 trainees were required to take physical education five days per week, while the civilian students continued the traditional prescription of three days per week.

Owing to the fact that civilian and V–12 students took physical education in Columbia College concurrently, and from the same instructional staff, a comparison of the two groups was possible. The result of this comparison was a source of enlightenment to the Department of Physical Education. Experience with the two groups has shown that a much greater degree of physical fitness can be attained when students attend classes five days per week, and also, that the psychological level of endurance can be raised. That is to say, healthy boys can do much more physical work of a body-developing type than they themselves think they can do. The Navy student is not, on the whole, unlike the average Columbia College student. A large proportion of the initial members of the V–12 unit assigned to Columbia were Columbia College students prior to their entering the Navy. When the Navy Standard Physical Fitness Test was given to civilians and V–12 students in July, 1943, the average McCall's T-score for both groups was not significantly different. The test results were: V–12 students, 41.7; civilian students, 39.3.

In November, after the Navy students had attended class five days per week and the civilian students three days per week—both groups for a period of sixteen weeks—the same students were retested. The Navy group during that interim increased the average score to 55, while during the same period the civilian group increased the average score to 43.6. Thus the total improvement of the Navy group was more than twice as great after attending class five days per week as was that of the civilian group after attending three days per week.

The optimum program should be based on a prescription of five periods per week for four years, but owing to limitations of space and equipment, our present antiquated plant rules out any program even approximating the ideal. It becomes necessary therefore to recommend a compromise—a type of prescription which can be conducted at Columbia pending the provision of facilities that are commensurate with our opportunities and our obligations.

With our present plant, together with such additions as could be made at Baker Field, a student body of normal size (1,800) can be given instruction and recreation as outlined in the following program:

1. A requirement for all lower college students (freshmen and sophomores) of three periods of physical education per week for two years.

2. A requirement for all upper college students (juniors and seniors) consisting of not less than one hundred periods of participation during the two-year period in diverse intramural, intercollegiate or recreational activities, with the stipulation that not more than sixty participation units shall be accepted for credit in any one year.

The credit recommended for this requirement will add one point for the completion of each year of the upper College prescription.

Activity Requirement. The continuation of medical examination to determine the health status of all students is indispensable to the safe operation of a program of physical education. All students who are organically fit to engage in vigorous activities would be given a battery of tests to determine their degree of strength, endurance, and coordination. If the test results show that a given student needs physical strength and endurance and would, therefore, profit little from sports and games, he would be required to take "basic" work for one school year. (Basic work would consist of muscle-building activities, such as apparatus, tumbling, calisthenics, running and swimming.) If, on the other hand, the test results of a student shows that he possesses adequate strength and endurance and a suitable degree of coordination, he would be permitted to elect activities in the "maintenance" program to meet the two-year period of formal class instruction. Each school year would be divided into quarters, and, at the conclusion of each of these six-week periods, new assignments to activities would be made. The required achievement with respect to activities in the maintenance program follows:

Two team games selected from basketball, baseball, football, crew, swimming, speedball, soccer, softball, volleyball, touch football, track, water games.

Swimming—minimum tests: 75 yards free style, 50 yards on back, plain dive.

One combative activity selected from boxing, wrestling, fencing.

Three individual recreative activities selected from badminton, bowling, golf, handball, squash, tennis.

Students who possess a high degree of skill in one or more sports, especially the more mature war veterans, would be permitted to demonstrate competence in any of the maintenance activities and thus to "achieve" that particular part of the requirement. This is not unlike the achievement test which is permitted in academic courses.

The Requirement of Students Participating in Intercollegiate Athletics. It is the opinion of the vast majority of physical educators that participation in intercollegiate athletics is of paramount value in the total development of college youth. The loyalty to a group, the intensity of work, the personal sacrifice for the good of the team, the give and take in body-contact games, the close association of athlete and coach, and the association with opponents from other institutions are experiences which are difficult—indeed impossible—to duplicate in formal class work. This Committee recommends therefore, that Columbia College follow the pattern of many leading institutions, and increase the scope of intercollegiate competition to include not only varsity and freshman teams, but also junior varsity in as many sports as possible. The construction, already authorized, of tennis courts and playing grounds at Baker Field, with bus transportation provided for the students, will serve as a relief from the crowded campus facilities until the projected new gymnasium is available.

The Department of Physical Education would permit a student to engage in intercollegiate athletics in lieu of the team-game requirements. Each student-athlete, however, will be required to pass the swimming test and to receive instruction in an out-door and an in-door recreational activity or demonstrate skill competence in such activities.

The requirement in physical education for the atypical group is of course subject to the careful consideration of a University physician. The medical officer prescribes the exact kind and amount of physical activity for each member of the group, and the Department of Physical Education holds atypical students responsible for only that portion of the normal requirement which is deemed by the Medical Service of the University to be in the interest of the students' future health and effectiveness.

The Requirement in Hygiene. Our present prescription of one semester hour in informational hygiene is an effort to present the minimum essentials of health information in the time allotted.

The topics we present and attempt to treat in fourteen hours are: biological introduction, sketching the development of the race and of the individual; science of foods and nutrition, including the chemical nature of foods, the functions of food and the bases of food selection; the muscular system and its vital relationships; the sexual aspect of life, embracing marriage and family relationships, the hygiene of marriage and methods of control and direction of the sexual impulse before marriage; and immunity and immunization, including the nature of disease-producing organisms, their means of access to the human body, and the serological measures for increasing resistance to their inroads.

7. The Upper Years

As STATED in the Report to the Faculty, Columbia College has been working towards an offering in the junior and senior years which will permit one of three educational choices, under advice: (a) specialization or (b) intensified study within two or three related fields, or (c) even broader acquaintance with the advanced reaches of the liberal arts. For these purposes, the College offers colloquiums, seminars, lecture courses, and readings courses.

College seminars, whether junior or senior, are conducted like their graduate prototypes: a small group of students attack a chosen problem within a given branch of study and present to the group their individual research on a phase of the problem. Discussion, criticism, and technical training are the main features of the common enterprise.

Lecture courses are what their name implies, though occasionally time is provided by the instructor for the discussion of related issues or for the clearing up of difficulties. Almost invariably, written work is required in addition to readings and examinations. Among such courses, those numbered from 1 to 100 are given for Columbia College undergraduates exclusively; if numbered in the 100s, they are jointly given for first-year graduate students and upper college undergraduates. Here are a few samples chosen at random from each group:

Fine Arts 67—Northern European painting. A study of painting in the north of Europe from the fifteenth to the seventeenth century. The discussion centers about the Flemish and Dutch masters from the van Eycks through Rembrandt, but also considers the French, German, and Spanish schools.

Music 58—Twentieth-century tendencies in music. Lectures and discussions of the idioms, aesthetics, forms, and styles of the chief contemporary composers.

Zoology 52—Elementary embryology. One hour lecture and four hours laboratory. Designed for general college students, for students of psychology, physiology, and geology, and those who intend to pursue zoology, botany, or medicine.

Anthropology 149–150—The American Indian. An ethnographic survey of North, Central, and South America, stressing the major physical, linguistic, and cultural patterns of New World civilization.

Chinese 131–132—Chinese literature. Survey of Chinese literature from the earliest times to the present, with emphasis on fiction, poetry, drama, and belles-lettres. The so-called canonical books, the moral, philosophical, and scientific treatises, are considered only in so far as they are necessary for the appreciation of the main subject matter of the course.

Geography b107—Industrial potentialities of Asia. A study of the economy of the Asiatic countries and of the impact of the West upon that economy with the introduction of modern industry and transportation. An examination is made of the geographic and economic factors contributing to Oriental industrialization and of the significance of that industrialization to the Western nations. Attention is given to the background of Japan's expansion to the mainland.

The colloquiums are characterized by the presence, in a small discussion group, of more than one instructor, the panel usually representing staff members from different fields. The type of these colloquiums is shown by the Colloquium on Important Books, described below (pp. 164 ff.).

Finally, the readings courses are for students who wish to read widely in a defined area, but without engaging in research (as in seminars) or in covering a subject or period (as in colloquiums). Courses in "Area studies" generally follow the readings course pattern as exemplified in the Columbia College readings course in American History, which is outlined below (pp. 172–175).

8. The Colloquium on Important Books

Historical. Much has been done in American higher education for college students of exceptional ability in specific fields; much, perhaps too much, has also been done for students who seem to have little or no ability in any field of study. For the latter, the road to learning or, at least, to a degree, has too often been leveled and graded, not to say degraded. The former group, undergraduates of marked competence in some or several academic disciplines, may in almost any University college pursue courses of postgraduate rank in their senior year or earlier if they have adequate preparation. Together with junior or senior seminars, these courses help the nascent historian or the incipient chemist to serve a valuable apprenticeship while still a member of the College. Thus properly qualified Columbia College students may take courses in the graduate schools of the University, and the exercise of professional options open the appropriate professional schools to undergraduates aspiring to become lawyers, physicians, engineers, or businessmen.

Meanwhile other students of exceptional ability whose intellectual interests are in the liberal arts tradition, have not always been equally well served. As early as 1916, Professor John Erskine, of the English Department in Columbia College, imparted to his fellow faculty members his concern for the spiritual and intellectual welfare of these students. The first result was the planning of the so-called "Erskine courses"—a series of two-year sequences in literature, philosophy, science, and history based on the great books of the Western world. The First World War postponed and changed the application of this forward-looking plan. History and philosophy were subsumed in the new Contemporary Civilization course of 1919, which was required of freshmen, not upperclassmen. This left the field clear for a junior and senior "Honors Course" in the great books, which was accordingly instituted under Professor Erskine's own direction, also in 1919.

Technique. The course was devoted to the reading and discussion of some fifty great books (listed below) with occasional sallies into music and the plastic arts when some concert or special exhibition provided the opportunity. The main work however was the weekly Wednesday evening discussion of a single masterpiece read in its entirety. The four groups, two in the junior year and two in the senior, consisted of some twelve students and two instructors—in all about fifty students, carefully selected and taught by a staff of eight.

For ten years the course continued on this plan, during which time it taught and trained the majority of those who later carried the Great Books idea to other institutions and expanded it into a whole curriculum. With the review of the upperclass college program at Columbia in 1929, the Honors course was suspended for two years, its place and performance studied anew, and then revived with slight modifications under the title of "Colloquium on Important Books." At the present time, it follows the selecting, grouping and staffing methods of the old Honors course without change. Students who have had Humanities A in their freshman year are entirely willing to reread some of the ancient classics in their junior year under different circumstances, which include their added maturity. The music and fine arts are, however, not dealt with, and the scientific classics are generally omitted, as needlessly encroaching on the work done either in Science A and B or in the course in the History of Science. Similarly, the introductory lectures, which for a time were required ahead of the reading assignment, have been abandoned.

The original "Erskine list," which continues to be in demand though the original syllabus is long out of print, was as follows:

Homer, *The Iliad; The Odyssey*
Herodotus, *History*
Thucydides, *History of the Peloponnesian War*
Aeschylus, *Prometheus, The House of Atreus*
Sophocles, *Oedipus Tyrannus; Oedipus Coloneus; Antigone; Electra*
Euripides, *Alcestis; Medea; Electra; Hippolytus*
Aristophanes, *The Frogs; The Clouds*
Greek Art: Percy Gardner, *Principles of Greek Art*
Plato, *The Symposium; The Republic; The Dialogues of Plato*
Aristotle, *The Ethics; The Poetics*
Lucretius, *De Rerum Natura*
Vergil, *Ecologues and Georgics; Aeneid*
Horace, *Odes; Epodes; Satires; Epistles*
Plutarch, *Lives*
Marcus Aurelius Antoninus, *To Himself*
St. Augustine, *The Confessions; The City of God*
The Song of Roland
The Nibelungenlied

St. Thomas Aquinas, *Of God and His Creatures*
Dante, *La Vita Nuova; La Divina Commedia*
Galileo, *Nuncius Siderius; On the Authority of Scripture in Philosophical Controversies; Four Dialogues on the Two Great Systems of the World; Two New Sciences, Third Day*
J. J. Fahie, *Galileo, His Life and Work*
Grotius, *The Rights of War and Peace*
Montaigne, *Essays*
Shakespeare, *Hamlet; Much Ado about Nothing*
Cervantes, *Don Quixote*
Francis Bacon, *The Advancement of Learning; The New Atlantis*
Descartes, *Discourse on Method*
Thomas Hobbes, *Leviathan*
John Milton, *Paradise Lost*
Molière, *Les Précieuses Ridicules; Le Bourgeois Gentilhomme; Le Misanthrope; Tartuffe; L'Avare*
George Meredith, *On Comedy and the Comic Spirit*
John Locke, *Essay Concerning Human Understanding*
Montesquieu, *The Spirit of the Laws*
Voltaire, *Candide; Toleration and Other Essays*
S. G. Tallentyre, *Voltaire in His Letters*
Jean-Jacques Rousseau, *Discourse on Inequality; Confessions*
Edward Gibbon, *History of the Decline and Fall of the Roman Empire*
Adam Smith, *The Wealth of Nations*
Immanuel Kant, *The Critique of Pure Reason*
Goethe, *Faust*
American State Papers: The Declaration of Independence; The Constitution of the United States; *The Federalist*
Victor Hugo, *Les Misérables*
Georg W. F. Hegel, *The Philosophy of History*
Sir Charles Lyell, *The Principles of Geology*
Balzac, *Old Goriot*

Thomas Malthus, *Essay on the Principle of Population* (parallel chapters from the first and second editions)
Jeremy Bentham, *An Introduction to the Principles of Morals and Legislation*
John Stuart Mill, *Autobiography; On Liberty*
Charles Darwin, *The Origin of Species; Autobiography*
Louis Pasteur: either René Vallery-Radot, *The Life of Pasteur,* or Emile Duclaux, *Pasteur, the History of a Mind*
Karl Marx, *The Communist Manifesto; Capital*
Lyof Tolstoy, *Anna Karénina*
Dostoevsky, *Crime and Punishment*
Friedrich Nietzsche, *Thus Spake Zarathustra; Beyond Good and Evil; The Dawn of Day* (Preface)
William James, *Psychology*

For any group of students, however competent, to undertake to master in two years the world's classics from Homer to William James seems an impossible task. For any group of instructors to undertake the teaching of such a course would appear to be overwhelming effrontery. Nor is the impossibility or the effrontery greatly reduced when it is admitted at once that this is in no sense a survey course, that no claim to completeness is made, and that the list of some one hundred twenty-five authors included in the present bibliography* is neither put forward as a complete roster of classic writers, nor is itself read in its entirety by the Colloquium groups. Twenty-eight to thirty authors are read in each of the two years of the Colloquium, one author in each week of the four semesters of the students' junior and senior years.

---

* *Classics of the Western World,* ed. by Alan W. Brown and Members of the Faculty of Columbia College, Chicago, American Library Association, 1943.

There is no expectation, no pretense, of doing justice to any of these authors in a week's reading and study. It may rather be said that we would do justice to our students in offering them a program of reading worthy of their fullest and continued application, that we would do justice to our own sense of educational values by concentrating attention on "the best that has been thought and said"—some of it, at least, certainly not all. Aristotle, Marcus Aurelius and Augustine, Montaigne, Shakespeare, Bacon, Descartes, and Jonathan Swift need no "justification" by us. It is rather we ourselves whose educational enterprises need to be justified, or at least tried, in the supreme court of their jurisdiction.

Within these limits, a very considerable part of such success as the course has had, has probably been due to the care with which students have been selected. Each applicant for enrollment is interviewed at the end of his sophomore year by a committee of members of the Colloquium staff. Though such an interview may seem something of an ordeal for the student, it has seemed to provide a reasonably effective method of selection when many complicated factors have to be considered. The various points of view and judgments of the committee members serve to check one another, and their impressions are amplified by careful examination of the applicant's previous academic record as well as by consultation with some of his former instructors and advisers. All this takes much time and not a little trouble, but it has proved itself well worth while.

The aim has not been to secure a standardized group of prodigies, nor to have a student body isolated from other groups on the campus by their esoteric preoccupations.

Though the Colloquium is offered for students of high academic standing, this has not been interpreted in a narrow sense by exclusive attention to previous course grades. Each applicant's interests are taken into consideration as well as his mastery of languages and competence in expression. The result has been a group of students of wide and varied outlook.

As the student group represents a variety of viewpoints and preparation, so the instructing staff is drawn from several cooperating departments. The staff has included representatives from the Departments of Classics, English and Comparative Literature, History, Economics, and Philosophy. It may be mentioned that of the eight members of the present Colloquium staff, six were associated with the former General Honors course—three as instructors, three as students.

Since the pair of instructors in each section act not as lecturers but as leaders of discussion, the pattern of an evening's performance is likely to be complicated, the design often remains obscure, and many threads are left hanging. Yet as the year progresses and the group's members become increasingly acquainted with one another, form and continuity may be increasingly discerned. For in a group working towards intellectual intimacy, many elementary considerations may gradually be taken for granted. Frequent references, which an outsider might find unintelligible, may in any meeting be made to previous discussions. At least in some of the groups this sort of association has been experienced as one of the welcome and excellent by-products of the Colloquium.

While gladly seeking to maintain the traditions of General Honors, we have felt free to depart from its precedents whenever this seemed desirable. Much was, of course, implied by the change of name and the elimination of the honorific aspects of the old title, and this change has apparently been an advantage. Students seem to be attracted to the Colloquium because of their interest in the contents and procedure of the course, without other motives suggested by a special honors degree and prestige.

The relationship of an undertaking like the Colloquium to specialized courses such as undergraduate seminars may be suggested by the distinction between educational specialization and concentration. In one sense, as noted above, the Colloquium has been an equivalent in the field of the humanities for what junior and senior seminars represent to students whose particular interests are in the field of the social sciences. There are, however, obvious differences. The work of the Colloquium is in no sense research. Nor does the Colloquium offer, except incidentally, training in methodology. It provides, rather, a direct and controlled experience of the works in which our tradition has been most fitly embodied.

9. A Readings Course in American History: 91A-92A

HISTORY 91A–92A was introduced in 1932 in connection with an upper-college course in recent United States history, for the purpose of remedying two of the characteristic deficiencies of the lecture-course method. It was designed, in the first place, to provide an opportunity for interested and superior students to read more extensively—or intensively—in the field covered by the lecture course than could normally be expected where programs included five or six separate electives. Secondly, it was conducted on the assumption that intellectual growth benefits from, even though it may not require, the stimulus of lively and informal discussion among compeers. Such discussion, to which the undergraduate has been introduced previously in Humanities and Contemporary Civilization, was necessarily more perfunctory in the larger lecture courses of the upper years.

By 1936, History 91A–92A had replaced the parent lecture course; and, with one brief interruption caused by the war, it has since carried a large part of the College work in American history above the elementary level. With the opening of a semester, students accepted for registration are formed into groups, each preferably consisting of from four to eight men, on the basis of interests and previous preparation. In a given term, for example, individual groups might be working on such varied subjects as United States relations with Latin America, the growth of corporations, the South since the Civil War, and the interrelations of economic, social, and political developments in the nation since 1890.

Each group, meeting in the instructor's office for two consecutive hours weekly, bases its discussions upon a prepared schedule of readings, which is subject to such later modification as may seem desirable. Grading depends upon effective participation in discussion and demonstrated competence in a term essay and an oral examination. Where interest and ability warrant, students are permitted to continue in the course for more than two semesters, or, occasionally and for double credit, to carry the work of two sections of the course concurrently. Advanced students, wishing to do original research, can arrange to take the course on a tutorial basis.

Inasmuch as the readings in History 91A–92A have been adapted to the needs of many kinds of upperclass groups over the past fifteen years, the two assignment schedules below are illustrative rather than "typical." With some variations, both have been used successfully a number of times with superior students.

I. The Progressive Movement

1. The Agrarian South and West after the Civil War
   Nevins, *Emergence of Modern America,* chap. 6
   Parrington, *Main Currents in American Thought,* III, 257–300
   Hicks, *Populist Revolt,* pp. 36–95
2. Monopoly, the Gospel of Wealth, and the Rise of Protest
   Tarbell, *Nationalizing of Industry,* chaps. 2, 5, 6, 12

Gabriel, *Course of American Democratic Thought,* chaps. 13, 17
Bellamy, *Looking Backward, passim*

3. The Farmer Organizes
   Hicks, pp. 96–273
4. The First Battle
   Hicks, pp. 274–423
   Sullivan, *Our Times,* I, chaps. 6, 9
5. The Progressive Movement in the States
   De Witt, *The Progressive Movement,* chaps. 10–12
   LaFollette, *Autobiography,* chaps. 4–8
6. The Progressive Movement in the Cities
   De Witt, chaps. 13–16
   Steffens, *Autobiography,* pp. 450–463
7. The Muckrakers
   Chamberlain, *Farewell to Reform,* chaps. 4–6
   Steffens, *Autobiography,* pp. 357–398
   Three "muckrake" articles
8. The Theodore Roosevelt Administration
   Pringle, *Theodore Roosevelt,* pp. 201–278, 339–371; 413–445, 476–494
   Bowers, *Beveridge and the Progressive Era,* pp. 223–236, 250–282
9. Thorstein Veblen
   Veblen, *Theory of Business Enterprise*
10. Taft and the Progressives
    Pringle, *William Howard Taft,* I, chaps. 21–22, 26–28
    Hechler, *Insurgency,* chaps. 1–7
11. The Republican Split
    Pringle, *Taft,* II, chaps. 39–42
    Pringle, *Roosevelt,* pp. 540–571
    Chamberlain, *Farewell to Reform,* chaps. 7–8

12. The Wilsonian Background
    Dodd, *Woodrow Wilson and His Work,* chaps. 1–3
    Kerney, *Political Education of Woodrow Wilson,* chaps. 2–11, 15
13. The New Freedom
    Baker, *Woodrow Wilson, Life and Letters,* III, chap. 7
    Paxson, *The Pre-War Years, 1913–1917,* chaps. 1–2, 4–6
14. Estimates
    Croly, *Progressive Democracy,* Introd., chaps. 8–11, 15
    Chamberlain, *Farewell to Reform,* chap. 9

II. Repercussions of American Life on Its Literature, 1915–1939

1. Brooks, "America's Coming of Age"
2. Dreiser, *An American Tragedy*
3. Anderson, *Winesburg, Ohio*
   Masters, *Spoon River Anthology*

4–5. Lewis, *Babbitt; Dodsworth; Arrowsmith*

6. T. S. Eliot, *Poems*
   Cummings, *The Enormous Room*

7–8. O'Neill, *Hairy Ape; Emperor Jones; Great God Brown; Desire under the Elms; Strange Interlude; Mourning Becomes Electra*

9–10. Hemingway, *Farewell to Arms; For Whom the Bell Tolls;* short stories

11. Caldwell, *God's Little Acre*
12. Dos Passos, *U.S.A.*
13. Frost, *Poems*
    Wilder, *Our Town*
14. Wolfe, *The Web and the Rock* or *You Can't Go Home Again*
15. Krutch, *The Modern Temper*